"The Black Veils is Father Sebastiaan's g... cinct guide to Vampire life, in all it's myst... be without this valuable handbook. As I lie in my lair and peruse The Black Veils, the Vampire World is illuminated and I feel sated with essential knowledge. Thank you, Father Sebastiaan!"
Laila Nabulsi, Producer of Fear and Loathing in Las Vegas

"Black Veils is engaging with its other worldly sensibilities in a unique thought provoking atmosphere."
G Tom Mac, singer / songwriter Cry Little Sister, theme song of Lost Boys

"In Black Veils, Father Sebastiaan, who has been a leader in the vampire community for a quarter of a century, presents a summary of his wisdom gained from interacting with the new vampires in our midst, especially as it relates to the individual vampire' own positive self-development and the ethical dimension of vampire life. Black Veils is essential reading for anyone wanting to know more about both the spiritual and secular dimensions of modern vampire existence."
J. Gordon Melton, Professor of American Religious History Baylor University

"An amazing piece of work. From Fledgling to Elder to ancient f**ks like me, there is something here for everyone."
Lord Chaz, Vampire Street Theatre, Master Storyteller, New Orleans

"Since I meet Father Sebastian in 1994, I've watched the culture and empire of Vampires grow to vast numbers world wide. I've read all his prior books & Black Veils is a must read for all those romanticizing the darkness. It answers questions pertaining to the vampire terms, codes, morals and way of life... or undead life. Black Veils is yet another grand addition for night stalkers to absorb, thus providing knowledge to all pointy teeth millennials on the age of modern Vampirism."
Myke Hideous / Sabretooth Ancient (Brood of 1995), Founder of The Empire Hideous

"The Black Veils is a unique book for both the experienced and the enthusiast. One can truly adapt the concepts of this book in their daily life and use each Black Veil as an inspiration to become the more enlightened, more vampiric version of oneself."
Mahafsoun, YouTube Personality and Alternative Model

"I am loving my journey into Father Sebastiaan's Black Veils. The vampire lexicon is a rather new world to me and he makes it clear, enticing, romantic and magickal. A must-read for those entering or in the vampire culture!"
Patti Negri, Witch of West Hollywood / Ghost Adventures

"The Black Veils really nails it on the head. A must read for anyone thats interested in joining the vampire culture or just curious. Also, beautifully bound and a great add to any vampire book collection."
Ashley Pagliuso, Straight out of the Coffin

"Father Sebastian steps forward and reveals his original testament. Were you born with the Black Veils already with you? Read and find out."
Voodoo Queen Bloody Mary, New Orleans Haunted Museum / Ghost Adventures

"The Black Veils have arrived in Transylvania! A special book that will change and positively inspire the Vampires all around the world. Each Veil serves to make this book a unique lexicon perfectly adapted for the modern society."
Andrea Bathory, Special Events Director Bran Castle, Bran Romania

"A tome for the times as many awaken to their true potential as an embodiment of the living Vampire. As you pore through this book, page by page, you will begin to unveil aspects of your true nature, illuminating the infinite expanse of potential that stretches out before you."
Kaedrich - Author Runes of Transformation

"Father Sebastiaan has proven time and again to be the quintessential leading force within The Vampire Community, «Black Veils» is proof of that nomen. With over 200 pages of definitive lore that reaches from beyond the basic conventions of modern vampire society to the obscure inner workings of the privileged few, «Black Veils» will be hailed as a triumph of the culture and a standard of excellence. It's single greatest achievement is in its accessibility to all, whether this is your first time experiencing the culture or you are a long time devotee, this finely crafted piece of literature will seamlessly bridge the two, in one singular unifying expression of all things vampiric."
Drake Mefestta - Shadow Emporium - Apothecary and Shoppe

"A further reach towards the fine tuning of our immortality"
Anthony "DJ ShocktheMonster" & The Buzzfeed Vampire

"The Black Veils is well researched as it is strikingly beautiful, fitting for the theme of the book. Concise and informative, it is a great addition to ones library on the subject."
E.R. Vernor, Author of Vampires a World History

"Dark, intriguing and sinfully DELICIOUS."
Leonardo Cavallero, Master Fangsmith of San Diego

"I have been a Fangsmith for over 15 years endorsed and supported by Sabretooth Clan and I count Father Sebastiaan as the Founding Father of the world wide Vampire Culture. And this book is indeed the next step."
Robbie Drake, the Fangsmith of London

THE DAYSIDE & NIGHTSIDE

Within the Vampire Culture (VC) and community there are traditionally two primary paradigms: the Dayside (mundane, profane and "normal" world) and Nightside (spiritual, metaphysical and "vampire" world.) This concept was created by the Temple of the Vampire (TOV) and has been adopted over the years into the majority of the Vampire Community (VC) as standard terminology. This book is firmly rooted in understanding the difference and balance between the Dayside and Nightside paradigms as described within the Black Veils.

VAMPIRE VS. VAMPYRE

This book spells Vampire with an "I." In my previous books I have used the older Victorian spelling of Vampyre with a "y." This originally differentiated lifestyle from literature, fiction, legend, and fantasy, but those lines are now blurred. Old schoolers still use the old Vampyre spelling, but the new generation spells Vampire with an "i."

This copy of BLACK VEILS was formally consecrated on _____ (date) *and is the property of*

_____
(Nightside Name)

3

WEBSITE REFERENCES

Sabretooth Clan
www.sabretoothclan.com

Father Sebastiaan
www.fathersebastiaan.com

Endless Night Vampire Ball
www.endlessnight.com

Vampire World Documentary
www.vampireworld.com

Black Veils

THE VAMPIRE LEXICON

ENGLISH OUTER COURT Edition

FATHER SEBASTIAAN
FOREWORD BY ROSEMARY ELLEN GUILEY

sabretooth

black veils
THE VAMPIRE LEXICON
English OUTER COURT Edition

June 21st 2018

ISBN #: 978-0-578-18612-2

First Printing, English

Cover & Interior Artwork: William Vocant
Forward by: Rosemary Ellen Guiley
Original Vampire Ankh Design: D'Drennan
Contributions by: Victor Magnus
Special Editorial Thanks: Frejya, Ruth Waltz, Marcel Curiel, Declan, Celtic Shadow

Printed in the United States of America.

THIS BOOK IS DEDICATED TO ALL MY CHILDREN.
BOTH SABRETOOTH AND THROUGHOUT THE EXTENDED LEGACY.
LOVE & LOYALTY.

table of contents

Foreword

By ROSEMARY ELLEN GUILEY

What does it mean to live as a vampire? There are no simple answers to that question. Modern vampirism is a fairly new field with a great deal of unexplored terrain. Whether you skim the surface of it or plunge deep into it as part of your identity, vampirism is a process of discovery. Adventurers need maps and tools, and this book, the Black Veils, is your ultimate guide into the mystery.

When I began research on my first book on vampires, Vampires Among Us, in the 1980s, I found a much different vampire subculture than exists now. In fact, there wasn't much of one at all. Vampire: The Masquerade had yet to make the scene, and the secret vampire underground of clubs and groups was loosely organized and largely unknown. The Sabretooth Clan had yet to be born. The Anne Rice vampires were making an impact, but by and large, those who called themselves vampires or who wanted to be vampires were wandering in limbo. They had no guides, no models, no handbooks. They had only what they saw on the screen and read in novels. So, many of them dressed in Dracula capes, slept in coffins, avoided sunlight, crosses, and garlic, attempted to drink blood, and looked for "real" vampires to turn them.

As vampires found each other and banded together, one individual emerged to do more than any other to define, shape, and direct the "new vampire": Father Sebastiaan. From the beginning of his involvement in the vampire culture in the early 1990s, Father Sebastiaan recognized the deep mystical nature of vampirism and saw how to mold it into something sophisticated and even spiritualized. Vampirism was much more than whether one drank blood or life-force energy, or adopted the attributes of fictionalized vampires. Father Sebastiaan saw vampirism as a defining way of life and as an art form, with codes of honor, ethics, and values.

Vampire ethics may strike the outside observer as a contradiction, but the modern vampire is a far cry from the wretched, reviled creature of centuries past. Dead or alive – and there are many old traditions of living vampires around the world – the vampire of old was a feared, unholy outcast. Those predators upon the living still exist, but the new vampire culture has become something much different and more complex, and with the ability to profoundly affect the course of a person's life.

Father Sebastiaan developed a new mythos for modern vampirism, a way to achieve higher consciousness and immortality, and along the way live in power, grace, and elegance. This mythos has formed the Vampire Archetype.

What exactly is the Vampire Archetype? It is a governing force and the model blueprint of modern vampirism. Archetypes are ancient. They are universal primordial images that have been passed down from an ancestral past that includes not only early man but man's prehuman and animal ancestors – perhaps the very origins of vampirism itself. Archetypes are not part of conscious thought, but are predispositions toward certain behaviors patterns. They embody qualities both positive and negative, and they are modified by collective human behavior. Everyone who participates in the Vampire Culture contributes to the Vampire Archetype.

Carl G. Jung further developed the concept of archetypes, but did not originate it – ideas about archetypes go back to classical Greek philosophers such as Plato. Anything can be an archetype, and they are found in myth and folk tales. For example, the "hero" is an archetype, as is the "fool," the "king," the "queen," and so on. Archetypes are endless, and anything can become an archetype.

The Vampire Archetype is multi-faceted, embodying beliefs and fears from the collective human experience over centuries past, combined with modern beliefs that have arisen in the vampire subculture as it evolves and defines itself.

The dark, negative side of the Vampire Archetype is readily seen in accounts from earlier times, and in early fiction and drama portrayals. The negative vampire is predatory, a taker of the life force without regard to its victims. It is unwanted and reviled.

The vampire subculture has brought out the positive side of the Vampire Archetype. This aspect of the vampire is ennobled and empowered. Power is used for self-preservation and self-determination, but not at careless expense to others. Attention is paid to spiritual development, legacy, and the governing structures of the vampire community. The empowered and aware vampire may remain aloof from others by choice, but possesses the skill to integrate into mainstream society. Adopting the elements of the Vampire Archetype amounts to a rebirth or identity for many people.

There are four main archetypes that play significant roles in human personality and behavior, and we can see them as parts of the Vampire Archetype as well. They are:

THE PERSONA, which is the public mask or "outward face" behind which a person lives, in accordance with the expectations of society. Individuals may have a collection of masks to meet various social situations. Vampires wear multiple masks. They have dayside masks for interacting with the public and society, which keep their vampire nature secret. They have nightside masks, perhaps several, for different vampire activities and relationships.

THE SHADOW, which is the inferior, other side of a person. The shadow is uncivilized and desires to do that which is not allowed by the persona. For vampires, the shadow expresses the dark side of the Vampire Archetype – unbridled, raw, and even destructive power. The predatory nature of vampirism is not ignored or repressed, but embraced as part of the lifestyle of power. By definition, vampires are takers – most of them take the life-force from others, and some take blood. The modern vampire is not wild and out of control, a danger to society, but instead learns how to pursue this nature in ways sanctioned by the larger community. The primal side of vampirism is acknowledged and honored.

THE ANIMA AND ANIMUS, which are the male and female sides of the psyche, respectively. Every person has qualities of both sexes which enable a full range of expressions. Cultural conditioning, however, often molds individuals to deny their opposite sexual nature. The Vampire Archetype encourages individuals to be balanced and express both sides of their nature. Emotion in men is not a sign of weakness; assertiveness is not unbecoming in women. This free expression applies to sexuality as well.

The self, which is the organizing principle of the personality. It exists apart from the ego, and unites the conscious and the unconscious. It fosters an awareness of the interpenetration of all life and energies in the cosmos. The empowered vampire, through application of values, spiritual laws, and the tenets of the vampire community, gains a confident sense of place and purpose in the greater scheme of creation.

The new *Black Veils* is the most significant guide to vampire ethics, living, and conduct in publication. In 100+ entries, it defines terms, concepts, and relationships, and set forth guidelines for the proper and desired behavior. It is an indispensable book for both new and experienced vampires.

Society is badly in need of a restoration of ethics and etiquette. We are losing ground by the day to sloppy attitudes, rude behavior, clothing that reveals a profound lack of respect, both for self and society, and more. By no means do we need to return to the stiff and oppressive rules of earlier times. Rather, Father Sebastiaan calls upon the modern vampire to be a model for others. Men are gentlemen and women are ladies, with no loss of independence and free will. Strength of character is cultivated, as is the freedom to reinvent yourself.

Through the *Black Veils*, you will learn what it means to tap into the Current, a stream of creative, inspirational, and spiritual energy that fuels the Vampire Archetype. There is a profound mystery to the Current that cannot be specifically defined, but must be experienced to be known and understood. The Current is one of the Great Mysteries of the Vampire Archetype.

The *Black Veils* is the orienting compass in all areas of the vampire life. Vampires are quite diverse in their interests and engagement in the vampire life, but no matter where you start or how deep you want to go, the *Black Veils* will show you the way.

Father of the Sabretooth Clan and Impresario of the Endless Night Vampire Ball. I have been involved in the vampire community since 1992. Many consider me, whether they love me or hate me, the "founding father" of the modern Vampire Culture.

This book is about the positive and empowering elements of the secrets, mysteries and methods of Vampirism that I discovered over my years in the Vampire World. Within, you will find a celebration and exploration of the positive elements of the Vampire Archetype: immortality, love, elegance, mystery, decadence, passion, self empowerment, exploring art, culture, good health, and embracing our primal nature. The negative elements of the Vampire Archetype are rejected, including misery, torture, murder, depression, criminal activities, being cursed, self-destructiveness, and narrow mindedness. Take the elements that resonate with you and leave the rest. Every culture in history has a Vampire mythology; the Western modern world knows Dracula, Lestat, Edward, Bill, and Erik. The lines of reality have been changed and blurred so fantasy manifests as a reality through the Black Veils.

Just reading this Black Veils will not make you a Vampire, nor will it ask you to drink blood, have you sleep in a coffin, let you shape shift into a wolf, or promise you guaranteed immortality. However, it will challenge and inspire you to test and explore how elements of the Vampire mysteries can be applied to and empower your life.

This book was originally inspired by my interactions with the Current of energy I witnessed amongst my various fang clients, be they lovers of Vampire fashion, art, fiction, literature and entertainment, or involved more in other aspects of the Vampire lifestyle.

In 2007 I read a book called The Secret that made many things clear.

Since 1995 when I founded Sabretooth Clan as a "fangclub" for my personal fang clients, elements of this law fueled the collective spirit of the clan, which seemed unexplainable in lay terms at the time. I began to connect dots and noticed an elegant, dedicated, sincere, beautiful yet primal and draconian commonality of those drawn to me to obtain fangs. Like attracts like; throughout Black Veils you will discover many aspects of the Law of Attraction at work within "Sabretooth Clan" traditions, agreements, and perspectives.

Through the Art of Fangsmithing (which is best done in person,) I have witnessed personal connections and experiences with the Law of Attraction through intimate interactions with those who are drawn to the Vampire archetype. This took nearly two decades of traveling Europe and America as a Fangsmith, meeting clients one-on-one and seeing their eyes shift as they got their first look at their "transformation". Together we are building our fanged culture.

The "Current" is a spontaneous collective of ideas, agreement, spirituality, philosophy, traditions, and experiences. This Current comprises a series of philosophies, teachings, and traditions that are common to these individuals. While on the other side of the coin, the "Legacy" is the story of my fang business and those it has affected. I have carefully kept my own notes and recently formally composed them into what I now call THE BLACK VEILS. Each Veil is a teaching and begins with a simple word of power, then a precise definition and a clear description relating to the Vampire Current.

The reality is that I have met more people who identify with the Vampire archetype and had intimate experiences with them through my in-person fangsmithing than anyone else alive today. This is a fact, not just a narcissistic statement.

The vast majority of people who come to me for fangs do not consider themselves "real vampires". Yet for some reason, be it spiritually or through some sheer piece of luck, they have ended up on my "fang throne" (client's chair) with my hands shaping fangs in their mouth. Through this transformative experience they become touched by, reaffirmed to, or awakened to the Vampire Current. There is no limit to who they may be - they may be your neighbor, schoolteacher, a relative, or even your mailman! By day they often live a normal quiet life, but at night or on holidays like Halloween, they indulge and revel in their secret life as they don their fangs and go out to gathering such as banquets, Vampire balls, nightclubs, Vampire theatres, or their local Vampire meet up. Many have traveled across the world to meet others of like mind and to get their fangs made. Clients have gone so far as to travel to Paris from Rio and from Germany to New York to fit into my crazy schedule. What differentiates my clients from the "online Vampire community" is that they strive to gather in person, not just over the web, and come together to meet others of like mind face to face to celebrate the Current.

What few realize is that the Vampire Archetype is rife with forbidden desires such as like sexual sadism and other taboos. Modern life has so ingrained these things into our popular culture that image of the Vampire has become an outlet for such taboos. The Vampire relates to our more primal nature and simultaneously our deepest desires for immortality, romance, love, magic, decadence, mystery, and elegance. The collective of all the varied "Vampire Tribes" has fueled the Vampire Current, and my goal is to capture and clarify these mysteries to create applications for everyday life. Through exposure to the concepts of the elementary Vampire Mysteries within these Black Veils, many find that some manifestation of these taboos can benefit them in their lives. Many consider learning these concepts a rebirth, awakening, or reaffirmation of what they already know, accepting the positive elements of this immortal Vampire archetype and rejecting the negative traits.

For years I resisted writing the complete Black Veils. However, now with the rebirth of the Sabretooth Clan in its "old school" but still modern incarnation, seeing these Veils in print has become an experiment; now is the right time. Not all of these Black Veils are present in every person I make fangs for; however most of my fang clients will strongly relate to many as strong aspects of their personality. Many will begin to manifest these characteristics once they go through the Rite of the Transformation, which is the experience of the client looking into the mirror for the first time after getting their first pair of fangs. I cannot explain why the Vampire Current has emerged or how it manifests, it seems to be spontaneous.. I do know that there is a subtle current which unites and binds my clients to me and others like us. When two fang clients meet and discover that I made their fangs, there is almost always an immediate familiarity and fraternity. You would be surprised how many of what I call my "fang grandchildren" I have because of clients meeting at one of my parties or just hanging out in one of my shops, forming a relationship, and then having children to create their own family.

Many of my clients consider getting Sabretooth fangs to be a spiritual Rite of Passage. This is often the birth of a new identity or self-image for someone and I feel honored to witness this every time I make a set of fangs in my many travels. Even those who have never heard of the craft of fangsmithing and spontaneously get fangs by walking into a concert or a Halloween store are usually shocked to notice a change in their life. My theory is that the Vampire Current was always within them and was finally awakened. From my experience it is better not to ask "why" and instead to simply enjoy sharing the process of picking and choosing of these elemental Veils that each individual relates to. This is the Law of Attraction at work.

Many people may admire any or all of the Black Veils, but just a few have the potential and the awareness to fully realize the secrets contained within them. There are many interpretations of Vampirism and this book only seeks to explore one perspective. It is a perspective defined and lived by the Sabretooth Clan and by sharing it with others we hope to inspire many. When we refer to "Vampires" within this text, we are specifically speaking about those who embrace or are touched by the Vampire Current as explained in this book.

So, as you read this book, keep an open mind and ask yourself the following questions. Do Vampires truly exist? Are these words some sort of suggestion or hint? Does the Law of Attraction truly exist? Which of the Black Veils, these Vampire Virtues, do you most relate to?

Eternally,
Father Sebastiaan
Founding Father / Master Fangsmith : Sabretooth Clan
Impresario : Endless Night Vampire Ball

Origins of the Black Veils

By VICTOR MAGNUS

The Black Veils began as the rules and code of conduct of the legendary event Long Black Veil (LBV), which ran every Thursday at the MOTHER nightclub in Gotham Halo (New York City) from March 1997 to June 2000. Much of what we consider the modern Vampire Community, culture, traditions and philosophies were founded within hallowed walls of LBV by the Sabretooth Clan, which ran the event.

The original Black Veils of Long Black Veil were simple and included *"What happens in LBV stays in LBV," "18 to enter, 21 to feed (drink)," "All Vampires shall be Ladies and Gentlemen within the walls of LBV"* and *"Come in Dress Code, Fangs and Legacy Ankhs preferred."*

The concept for Black Veils were inspired by Renaissance Faire etiquette, the rules of The Eulenspiegel Society (TES) BDSM organization and applying elements of the vampire mythos to real life in application. The Black Veils were also intended to be a real life version of the traditions of the role-playing game: Vampire: The Masquerade. This was because many in the VC (Vampire Community) at that time were already using terminology from V: TM.

In late 1998 Michelle Belanger worked with Father Sebastiaan to expand the Black Veils for use beyond the LBV event into what became known as "Thirteen Rules of the Community." However, there was resistance from the VC because many felt that it was too derivative of the V:TM role-playing game. Once again, it was revised into seven basic guidelines, which was more publicly accepted by the VC.

Father Sebastiaan always thought the Black Veils as a philosophy and a "vampire bible" for the Legacy, however it was never truly complete. Finally in 2010 he had a realization, that the Black Veils were the core of the Sabretooth Clan culture, traditions, philosophy and culture. It was time to bring things home under one name, prepare them for the future of the Legacy and to solidify all my research and knowledge back under one banner. So this edition of the Black Veils is what he had envisioned things to be, coming full circle. This book is what he wanted to say from the beginning of his experience in the Vampire world. This is a massive revision of the Red and Purple Veils editions and a result of the visions and whisperings that he is truly in his heart to say have brought us to this point together.

So here they are, the Black Veils as they were intended to be.

Victor Magnus
Brood of 1995
Gatekeeper : Endless Night Vampire Ball
Mradu Magister : Sabretooth Clan

How to Read this book

Many people ask. "How do I read The Black Veils?" Well the answer is a secret known to the Sabretooth Clan and revealed here. This is called the "Oracle," which is a part of the Rites of Transformation when getting fangs. Start with going to the Table of Contents in this book and go through the list of Veils, feel it out and choose your favorite one. Then go read it and meditate on it. Once that is done read the following 23 starter Veils:

Xepher
Awakenings
Vampire Philosophy
Current (see appendix)
Pulses (see appendix)
Sabretooths
Black Veils
Bloodbath
Ankh
Black
Legacy
Courts
Elegance
Fangs
Fledglings
Magic
Howl
Dayside
Nightside
Love
Loyalty
Witch

Real Vampire F.A.Q.

This FAQ should be the first item read by newcomers to the Vampire culture. It is essential foundation information; the core of the Vampire Culture.

Are Vampires Real?

Yes, but not in the ways you may think. Living "Real" Vampires are human beings with a higher energetic need for vital life force (Chi, Prana, Mana, Ki) than the average human. If this Need goes unfulfilled, the Vampire experiences lower states of spiritual, physical, and emotional wellbeing. In order to sate this need, one must learn ethical techniques of gathering excess energy (called "feeding"). Vampires are usually divided into the categories of LIFESTYLE, PSYCHIC (energy) and SANGUINE (blood), but this often leads to misconceptions. A better terminology separates them into awakened and unawakened. All Vampires can practice just energy feeding. Lifestylers may practice a philosophy or employ the imagery, but are not all energetically Awakened. We also recognize Sympathetic Psychic Vampirism, a temporary Need resulting from a donor being depleted after being fed upon too much and for too long.

What is an Awakening?

Awakening is the revelation and understanding of one's nature as a Vampire, and also of one's energetic Need. Most Vampires are not born Awakened; they must have a revelation or experience to trigger the first stages of Awakening. The Awakening is not a singular event, but a cumulative process of smaller awakenings as the Vampire develops and learns. Being newly Awakened can be a difficult time and is often a solitary journey.

What are Lifestylers?

Lifestylers are individuals who embrace and incorporate the Vampire archetype into their lifestyle. Some are Unawakened or Awakened Vampires, yet most are not. Many are also Black Swans. These love the Vampire aesthetic and embrace elements of the mythology in their lifestyle, fashion, and mannerisms. Like the goths, they have their own subculture, social codes, events, and gatherings.

What is a Black Swan?

Black Swans are friends, lovers, family, and others who are open, friendly, and accepting or involved in the Vampire lifestyle, subculture and culture, but do not directly identify as Awakened Vampires. They can be lifestyle vampires or mundanes ("normal" folk), and can often (but not always) be consensual donors.

Can a Vampire "Turn me?"

Certainly not. The individual must have dormant potential, which the Vampire is most often born with. A deep communion (exchange of energies) between an Awakened Vampire and an Unawakened may trigger an Awakening in someone with potential.

Can Vampires Shapeshift?

Not physically. Like everyone, Vampires are bound by the laws of physics in the "Dayside" world. However those awakened to the metaphysical and spiritual "Nightside" world take many forms of astral shapeshifting, becoming wolves, felines, and even mist. This phenomenon is akin to the totem in shamanistic traditions.

Are Vampires at War with Werewolves?

No. This idea was introduced to the Vampire Mythos through the World of Darkness roleplaying games <u>Vampire: the Masquerade</u> and <u>Werewolf: the Apocalypse</u> by White Wolf Game Studio, in the early 1990s. It later appeared in <u>Twilight</u> and <u>Underworld</u> films. Werewolf mythologies are entirely different from Vampire mythology, and modern Vampire culture often calls Werewolves "Therians." Some traditions include spiritual and astral shapeshifting, often using the term "Lycanthropy."

Are All Vampires Evil?

No. Just like humans there are good people and bad people. Most modern Vampire cultures are built on honor, safety, respect, and consent. However, like any group of individuals, each member brings his or her own principles and perspectives.

Do Real Vampires Actually Feed?

Yes. Unawakened and Awakened Vampires must feed on vital life-force to fulfill their energy Needs. Unawakened feed unconsciously and without training or discipline, draining those around them emotionally. Awakened and properly trained Vampires learn to feed ethically and with discipline. There are three basic levels of feeding: Ambient, Surface and Deep. We list Sanguine or blood feeding but must clarify that it is a technique, not a level of feeding.

AMBIENT draws from life force radiated in a cloud around a group of people, such as a concert, sporting event, busy city street, night club, or shopping mall.

SURFACE OR TACTILE feeding draws from the outer layers of a donor's aura and is not invasive. It can be done by touch, or even at a distance.

DEEP feeding taps the core of a donor's energy body, and requires consent. It can be done through sex, or using reiki-like techniques. Deep feeding usually creates strong links between the Vampire and donor, which may be undesirable.

SANGUINE (BLOOD) is a type of deep feeding and always has major risks. This method is often used by Vampires undisciplined in the three energetic (psi) feeding techniques.

Can Vampires Fly?

Not physically (except in a hang glider or airplane like any other human). But many Nightside metaphysical, spiritual, and esoteric traditions of vampirism practice astral projection or out of body experiences (OBE).

Is Vampirism a Religion?

Not generally. Vampires hail from many spiritual and religious backgrounds ranging from agnostics, atheists, pagans, Christians, Catholics, Animists, Muslims, etc. Many spiritual and religious organizations practice Vampirism within their esoteric/spiritual traditions and philosophies.

Do Vampires Worship Satan or Lucifer?

Most do not. Satan and Lucifer are Judeo-Christian concepts and

Vampires are free to believe what they wish about them. Some Vampires are Satanists or Luciferians. Some are atheists. Many Vampires love the symbolism of Satan in rock & roll but don't worship him. Since Vampirism is not a religion, the concept of what Vampires "worship" is irrelevant.

ARE ALL VAMPIRES GOTHS?

No. Not all goths are Vampires and not all Vampires are goths. Although many Vampires enjoy the accepting nature of the gothic scene, it is more about music and aesthetics, making it very attractive to lifestyle Vampires for social purposes.

WHAT IS COMMUNION?

Unlike energy feeding, Communion is an exchange of energy between two or more Vampires and/or donors. While feeding is a one-way act to benefit the Vampire, Communion is a mutual feeding that creates a cycle of energy among all participants. Communion can be used to raise or clear energy or during tantric sex magic.

ARE VAMPIRES KILLED BY SUNLIGHT?

No. Vampires can go out in the day like any human. Some claim to be sensitive to sunlight and get headaches including migraines. Many Vampires are naturally night owls, and prefer to be actively nocturnal.

DO VAMPIRES HAVE HYPNOTIC POWERS OR SUPERNATURAL PRESENCE?

Not naturally, but many have natural charisma or "radiance" that outshines the average human. Some Vampires practice mentalism, NLP (neurolinguistic programming.) and social dynamics; practices often used by stage magicians. Vampires call application of these skills "Glamour" and "Projecting." Many also learn practices of seduction to aid in feeding. These are not supernatural powers and are strictly within the realm of illusion, psychology, and sociology.

DO VAMPIRES NEED TO DRINK REAL BLOOD?

No. According to modern psychology and scientific research, no human needs to drink blood to survive. The physical risks of contracting blood borne diseases (HIV, Hepatitis, etc.) and legalities (in some places only phlebotomists and medical care professionals can legally draw human blood) are clear concerns. However, some Vampires, known as Sanguines, believe they need to drink small quantities of human blood to survive or at least balance their emotional, physical, and spiritual health. Some Sanguines believe drinking blood gives them life-force. Most Sanguines seek consensual donors and employ strict safety practices, such as testing for diseases and using highest quality medical safety techniques. Some Sanguine prefer only to have one donor at a time, using the process as a powerful bonding technique. DISCLAIMER: The Sabretooth Clan recognizes this practice as part of the VC but does not as an organization actively promote or endorse these activities / feeding techniques.

DO VAMPIRES HAVE ANY SUPERHUMAN POWERS?

No. Vampires have physical human bodies. They eat, sleep, breathe, and move about like any other human. They live and they die. They are limited by the constraints of normal human life.

ARE VAMPIRES IMMORTAL?

No. Living Vampires are not physically immortal. They are human, and as such they physically age just like every other mortal. Many Vampires are interested in developing technologies like cryonics (freezing the body), life-extension, cybernetics, mind to computer uploading, and research into curing aging. Some Vampires and vampiric orders believe in reincarnation, apotheosis (self-deification) and immortality, and that the soul can become an ascended being.

DO ALL VAMPIRES WEAR CAPES AND DRESS IN BLACK?

Most Vampires look like any other individual. They can be your postman, school teacher, Uber driver, or local butcher. Many Vampires believe wearing black gives them a sense of drawing energy to themselves, projecting a form of mastery (like judges, black belts in martial arts, and police officers), and of course exuding mystery. However, most follow their own fashion interests. Lifestylers living inside the Vampire subculture often dress theatrically in movie-inspired or couture style aesthetics, often inspired by designers such as Alexander McQueen or Jean Paul Gaultier.

Do All Vampires Practice the Occult, Rituals or Magic?

No. Not all Vampires practice the occult and magic. Awakened Vampires are generally highly energy sensitive, making them attracted to energy work, Wicca, Neo-Paganism, chaos magic, meditation, yoga, Hermeticism, Reiki, Tantra, Qi Gong, etc. Many varieties of rituals, ceremonies, and rites of passage are prevalent among the many spiritual and occult-minded clans, covens, traditions, and orders.

Are Vampires Affected by Silver?

Not at all. Quite to the contrary: most Vampires prefer silver for its reflective mirror-like aesthetic and its symbolic relationship to the moon and the night.

Do All Vampires Organize into Covens and Clans?

Not all. Most Vampires are highly individualistic and solitary by nature, yet they can still be very social at times. The age of the Internet and social media has created a host of groups, websites, and forums for Vampires to virtually gather and have discussions. There are many in-person meetups and social events world-wide for Vampires. Vampire covens, also known as "Houses," were very popular before the Internet, but have become less popular in modern times.

Do All Vampires Have Titles Like Lord, Count, etc.?

No. This is mostly seen in the Lifestyle Vampire Community, and is largely inspired by pop culture and roleplaying games such as Vampire: the Masquerade and TV shows like True Blood. Theatrical titles can be fun for glamour and fascination but have no relevance to the real practices or the energetic Need of Real Vampirism. Be cautious —some Lifestylers have taken the "Vampire Game of Thrones" (VGOT) too far and take their theatrical titles far too seriously. They are roleplaying, and there is usually no harm in a little imagination. "Elder" is not a formal title. Elders are more experienced and wiser Vampires who mentor younger Vampires (or aid in their Awakening). Job titles within an organization should remain as offices of duty, positions of leadership, or a measure of time served. They have no place outside their own order or clan, and are generally not acknowledged in the greater VC.   See the Black Veil of Titles for more detail on this subject.

ARE ALL VAMPIRES INTO BDSM?

Not all.   Many Vampires (especially Lifestylers) are involved in the consensual BDSM (bondage discipline sado-masochism) lifestyle because it fits their vision of the Vampire archetype. The core nature of Vampire/donor dynamic creates dominant and submissive roles, but this is not always expressed as BDSM. 50 Shades of Grey along with the mainstreaming and popularization of the BDSM lifestyle has brought greater acceptance of the Vampire Community.

DO ALL VAMPIRES WEAR FANGS?

Not all. Yet fangs are a symbol of the Vampire lifestyle, and having a set made is very much a rite of passage for many entering the community. Fangs are a connection to one's primal nature, a magic trick, a mask, and tool of seduction. Fangsmiths around the world (previously called "family dentists") make custom fangs for those who want them. Many fangsmiths are specially trained as SFX artists or dental technicians.

Absinthe

The Green Fairy, better known as absinthe, has a strong history within the Vampire Community and has now become a drink of choice outside of the Sabretooth Clan for the mainstream world. However, few actually know that it made its first major resurgence within the underground Vampire Subculture in the early 1990s. Absinthe marked its place in vampire imagery with the film "Bram Stoker's Dracula."

Many Vampires brewed unique versions of this drink for several years and would share it with close friends. In the 1990s some clan members began experimenting as underground brewers and sharing elixirs with exclusive and private sales within the Vampire Community.

To this day the Vampire absinthe ritual is a wonderful and secretive ceremony used to celebrate important events such as birthdays. Due to modifications in U.S. laws, true absinthe is now available for purchase in America. As absinthe is easily obtainable at many liquor stores, it makes it very convenient when you cannot find a genuine absinthe Alchemaster or Alchemistress in your area.

Adults

The Adults Black Veil represents an individual's responsibility toward minors. It is not advisable to include minors directly in the Vampire Community until they pass the age of majority, which in most of the Western world is eighteen years of age. Within the Sabretooth Clan involving minors in the Clan's internal cultre and activities is strictly forbidden.

What makes this so important is that minors are too young to have already established their own sense of individuality in the real world. In regards to acquiring custom fangs, their teeth are not yet mature enough under the age of majority to be properly fitted. Most children have dental corrective braces fitted between 12-15 years of age because their jaws are not yet fully settled.

This does not mean minors are not allowed at some family gatherings. Many social events such as trips to theme parks or to some music festivals may be open to them. However, attending Vampire meet ups and reading the Black Veils should be reserved for when they come of age and can make their own decisions legally and mentally. This is of course for their benefit. One might be able to teach them many of the virtues indirectly, such as through classes in philosophy, art programs, spiritual retreats, music classes, concerts, museum visits, rock concerts and so on.

Altars

Vampire altars are a central external focus for ritual, meditation, and magic. Most Vampire altars face west, to represent the Gates of the Dragon, Death and Rebirth.

Traditionally, an altar consists of a table covered with a black cloth. The items on the altar may include an ar'thana (black-hilted, double-edged blade), a decorated box to contain materials, a wooden wand (for directing Will), a speculum (black mirror for connecting to the Current), figurines and sigils representing different Pulses or deities, The Vampire Legacy Ankh, a cauldron or other apparatus for burning incense, photos of ancestors, candles (red, purple, silver and black), a Grimoire, a chalice, and Florida water for cleansing.

Most Vampires have a personal altar in their home, either hidden away in a private ritual chamber or openly displayed depending on their living situation. Altars are personal focus points of each Vampire and are highly personal, decorated and customized, reflecting the spirit, interests and perspectives of its owner. Looking at a personal altar is an interesting way to get to know another Vampire.

Amulets

hysical objects that are charged with the Current or another type of energy are known as amulets and talismans. The difference between an amulet and a talisman is that a talisman is charged with a very specific purpose. It can even have a servitor bound to it or be "programmed" with a sigil. Amulets are more generic in purpose.

Pendants bearing religious symbols, such as Pentagrams for Wiccans, Crosses for Christians, and Stars of David for the Jewish are generally amulets. They represent the individual's spiritual path. The Legacy Ankh represents the Legacy and the Black Veils. Legacy Ankh pendants begin as amulets. When formally consecrated and attuned to a specific individual, they become talismans forcing and amplifying the owner's Xepher.

Amulets and talismans imbued with the Current can be created by anyone who is properly trained in their making. Such items may include not just Legacy Ankh pendants, but also custom-made amulets and talismans with sigils and the Current imbued in them. Vampiric talismans are similar to "mojo bags" in other esoteric systems like Voudou.

Ankh

The ankh, or in Latin the crux ansata (cross with a handle), was originally the Egyptian hieroglyph which meant "life". Many ancient Egyptian artworks, especially funerary art, depict gods and pharaohs bearing this symbol. The ankh was also associated with Osiris, the god of death and rebirth, and ankhs were often placed with mummies in order to symbolically convey the gift of immortality. Over time the ankh came to symbolize immortality, and can even be seen as a key to unlock the gates of death. The Rosicrucians and members of Hermetic orders often use this symbol in their rituals. The Coptic Christians , as well, employed it as a symbol of life after death. Ankhs incorporating mirrors into their design have sometimes been used to symbolize perception of the subtle reality.

The bladed ankh first surfaced in popular culture in the 1983 film The Hunger, directed by Tony Scott and based on the novel by Whitley Strieber, who also, significantly, wrote the novel Communion. With its historical symbolism, cultural significance, and esoteric nature, the bladed ankh was the obvious and most common symbol for the Vampire.

See the Legacy Vampire Ankh in the appendix.

Anti-Discrimination

The Vampire Anti-Discrimination Veil is one of our most empowering strengths. One thing we know is the Current itself does not discriminate on whom it touches. The birth of this incarnation of the Current took place in the mid to late 1990s in one of the most diverse areas in the world, with every possible gender, orientation, ethnic, spiritual, national, social, religious, and cultural background living together in close proximity. This continues as an element of Vampire Anti-Discrimination.

Vampires are empowered through a unity, which few can understand, however the strength of this unity is diversity. We consider discrimination based upon someone's genetic makeup or where they were born as an insult to collective consciousness of the Current and a pure sign of basic ignorance. We support each other no matter what. Vampires are Vampires and we stand together against common issues and problems united in Family heritage. This is the powerful aspect of Vampirism which defines the Current.

Every human body bleeds red and with our human skins, upbringings and genetics, this Black Veil stands as a power that has always been a part of what we are. It is fine to fear the unknown, but it is evolution to understand it. This is what brings us forward in the world and is a key element of Xepher (vampire awakening).

Apotheosis

ampires both in action, mythology, legend, and archetype have the one common trait of being able to "escape" death either metaphorically or literally. Combined with their love and passion for Life, an immortalist perspective and a strong sense of individuality, this Black Veil puts forth the concept of personal godhood and divinity; known to the Ancient Greeks as Apotheosis.

Apotheosis is a common concept in the ancient cultures of Greece, but it is most notably recognizable in Heka, the Egyptian Mysteries. This can be seen as being related to such things as discovering the Elixir of Life or the search for the Philosopher's Stone in alchemical arts. Gnostic traditions often embrace the concept of Self-Deification in a more humble sense of surviving death and knowing divinity personally. Today Apotheosis can be visible in modern traditions such as Buddhism and LaVeyan Satanism.

Now this does not mean that the Vampire seeks to rule others or be in control of the entire world, it simply means that through full acceptance of this Black Veil they hold themselves as their own personal divine Self, thus worshipping the ego. Apotheosis in the Vampire sense is more about celebrating life and from the Dragon's perspective the ability to consider life and ego as almost divine. Vampires are notorious narcissists and this is the ultimate expression of that Black Veil.

Art

Vampire Art? You might think all Vampire Art has to be gothic, full of dark images and vampires flying through the night sky. Vampire Art, like "Vampire Sports," of course, is not what you would expect and even fangsmithing is considered an artistic endeavor amongst the Sabretooth Clan.

Vampires generally love many forms of art because they embody our love of history, creativity, and our secrets and mysteries. When visiting a new city, many Vampires will find themselves running to the local museum (like the Louvre in Paris or the Metropolitan Museum of Art in New York City), instead of rushing to the local Vampire Haven or meet up. Visiting museums is one of the best ways to taste the spirit of the local energy.

Regarding creativity: Vampires may include elements of the Legacy Ankh sigil, the Ouroboros or the Mirror into their own artistic designs with empowering symbolism the sigil brings them. Many Vampires love to draw flash art for tattoos, body paint, sculpture, airbrushing and the like. Art for the Vampire is about creativity and expression, especially when they create it themselves.

Ar'thana

The ar'thana is a black-hilted, double-edged knife or sword that represents the control of energy. Only members of the Priesthood who are presiding are permitted to wield it in group ritual. The ar'thana is NEVER used to draw physical blood. Its function is symbolic only. The ar'thana is similar in function and use to the Wiccan athame, which is used to channel and direct energies.

The word ar'thana comes from the same root of the Old French word for "dagger," Arthame. In addition to ritual use, the ar'thana can be used as a utility tool for cutting ropes and mixing herbs. Black-hilted, double-edged ritual knives can be found in the Key of Solomon and were made popular in a translation by S.L. Mathers of the Hermetic Order of the Golden Dawn.

Within the Black Veils, the ar'thana can be consecrated with the life-force of its owner. The consecration ritual for the ar'thana includes injecting life-force from the owner and the Current directly into it and then sealing it with a Name. This process creates an astral duplicate of the blade for use in the subtle reality.

Awakening

wakening is process that happens over time; a series of steps and not a single moment. When the Vampire Awakens, they realize they are truly a Vampire and fully acknowledge their calling to the Current. Within the Sabretooth Clan, "the Awakening" is the most important revelation. It comes when the Vampire looks into the mirror and see their fangs for the first time. This can be a major step of Xepher. Vampiric Awakening is similar to someone accepting their sexuality or a religious person finding their faith. Some jokingly call it "Born Again Vampires." This is considered a "Natural" and often results in many Ronin. The Vampire can only truly Awaken to the Nightside after they establish the Dayside philosophy as a personal path. Be Cautious: many individuals will feel the calling td rush to the Nightside and become lost or burned out.

The Awakening is an element of Xepher that is never truly over for a Vampire. The most difficult hurdles of the Nightside Awakening are often breaking the chains of mortalism and embracing Vampire Philosophy. Each individual Awakening is different. Some Vampires quickly embrace their nature and move forward, while other Vampires have a difficult time with various points of Xepher. There are many catalysts for Awakening. For some it happens spontaneously. Others are Awakened by being deeply fed upon by another Vampire or through applications of the Family Quest. Many are sponsored by a patron Ancestor who has subtly guided them throughout their process of awakening through dreams, visitations, and inspiration.

There comes a day when a Vampire can look at him/herself in the mirror with love and loyalty in their heritage and proudly state, "I AM A Vampire." There are many further points of Awakening; only those who "open their Vampire eyes" and see a reality hidden to the masses of the mundane discover these secrets.

Balls

ampire Balls are an intrinsic element of the Vampire Current, the ultimate place of celebrating the Black Veils. The most famous example of such an event is the Endless Night Vampire Ball. In answer to a person once asking what the Endless Night Vampire Ball was about, the answer was, *"The Endless Night Vampire Ball is like a Venetian Masque Ball meeting a Vampire Court, with the energy of a rock concert and the elegance of a burlesque cabaret!"*

The Endless Night Vampire Ball events began in 1996 with the intention of bringing the Vampire Ball model of event to the next level. They have inspired a style that mixes masquerade balls, pagan/esoteric gatherings, and fetish parties. These events, with a strict dress code, often have fire breathers, bands, DJs, ballroom and even tango/salsa music. One might be treated to Victorian and burlesque styles, belly dancing, as well as vendors selling unique wares. Vampire Balls are ceremonies and no self-respecting Vampire would dare to appear out of creative attire, be it self-made or a collection of articles they shopped for in anticipation of the next event. The producers maintain the integrity of the dress code for all guests, performers and staff.

Vampire Ball events have been held in many major cities throughout Europe and America. Many are secret events just for Vampires and their special guests; others welcome those who wish to celebrate with Vampires in style.

black

Black is said to be the primary color of the Vampire, but can such a cliché concept have a foundation in truth? The color black represents authority, elegance, mystery, silence, death, chaos, strength, fear, secrecy, power, darkness, and seriousness. We see this in the clothing of priests, judges, police officers, academic robes for graduates, and lawyers in many countries such as the UK and France. Black tuxedos are worn for formal "black tie" functions. Black is also the color the mundane associate with witches and sorcerers. "Black Magic" can be seen as symbolic of the unknown worlds, which is now known as science.

Those who wear black are often said to be makers of their own destinies. Black is a good conductor of energy because it absorbs all frequencies of light, even in the infrared spectrum. Black also functions to neutralize negative energies and thus is good for banishing, purification, bindings, defensive Magick, and acts as a protective shield.

Many groups throughout mundane culture consider the color black to to be a strong symbol. The Christian sect of the Cathers considered black to be a color of purification; black mirrors in esotericism are used for scrying; many societies are considered "black" when they are highly secretive, the bandana code of the gay community in the mid 20th century used black as a symbol of BDSM. Within Japanese culture, black is symbolic of experience, nobility, wisdom and age. Even in most martial arts, the top level of achievement being the "black belt." Black is a powerful projection and symbol of the Vampire beyond the clichés.

Black Swans

ithin the Veils, "Black Swans" are non-Vampire individuals who are intimately knowledgeable about the VC and are friendly to it. They are often involved in the Vampire subculture and associated with a Vampire, and can be friends, donors, dayside family members, lovers, or even potential Vampires yet to be awakened. The term Black Swan was coined at the New York City (Gotham Halo) Vampire nightclub Long Black Veil in 1997, for those who would bring their friends, parents, siblings, and lovers to the club.

One misconception within the Vampire World is that all Black Swans are donors. This is certainly very common, but it is not always the case. Many are even lifestyle Vampires who wear fangs, dress up, and know a great deal about the Vampire culture, philosophy, and traditions.. Often Black Swans are practicing the dayside elements of the Vampire lifestyle known as "lifestylers."

In contrast to Black Swans are "White Swans" who are against the Vampire lifestyle to varying degrees ranging from very hostile to just annoying. These individuals can range from a girlfriend, friend, sibling or parent who strongly mocks or dislikes the Vampire lifestyle. They often will say things like, "Why are you wearing fangs?" or "You are really only living in a fantasy world, so stop it."

Black Swans are to be treasured by Vampires and are strong allies. Treat them well and with respect, they are not pets but individuals with open minds and often resonate strongly with the Current and Vampire World. Even though the term originated in the Sabretooth Clan it has become used by the Vampire Community throughout the world.

Blood

"*Blood is the Life*" paraphrased from Leviticus 17:11, is one of the most common quotes from the Bible associated with Vampires. However amongst the Vampires of the Sabretooth Clan this term has a different meaning, which is that Blood represents the "Current" of the Family. Originally in the Old Days of the Family we used the term "sanguine." Now we refer to members of the Sabretooth Family as brothers and sisters, or more formally "sorors" and "fraters."

We are not talking about blood fetishism or blood drinking in these Black Veils since that is out of the scope of this text, but the symbolic and spiritual relationship of Family and kinship most Vampires feel.

The Sabretooth Clan does not officially condone the act drinking of human blood (sanguine feeding) within the Family and private / public events for the purposes of safety due to the high health risks.

BloodBath

The Bloodbath is a cocktail that is the staple of the Vampire Culture around the world, with reports of it being made in South America, Siberia, Japan, and Australia. The Bloodbath is a central Black Veil, but few know it's true history. It was created by Alchemistress Ambrosia of the Sabretooth Clan as the staple drink of the Legendary Vampire Club "Long Black Veil" in Gotham Halo (NYC.)

This drink was such a favorite of many of the Sabretooth Clan and guests of LBV over the years that they would empty bar stocks in one evening. Many Black Veil Vampires recall the old days at LBV with dozens of Victorian and leather clad Gents and Witches standing around slowly sipping from wine glasses of Bloodbaths them in the Versailles room of MOTHER.

The Bloodbath is traditionally made with 1/3 Chambord liquor, 1/3 cranberry juice and 1/3 red wine (preferably Cabernet), then put on ice, shaken like a Martini, and served in a chilled wine glass. There have been many variations, such as the New Orleans Bloodbath, which uses a hint of rum, or other versions which add grenadine, spices, or to share a Bloodbath with another Vampire is a great pleasure, especially while at a Vampire Ball, meetup, haven, or moot.

Burners

The Burners Black Veil takes its name from those Sabretooth Vampires who participate either directly or in the culture surrounding the annual Burning Man Festival, held in the middle of the Nevada desert every Labor Day weekend in a temporary city known as Black Rock City.

Burners are a neo-hippy movement which embraces concepts of radical self-reliance and radical self-expression, gifting, no spectators and immersive participation that comes from the Burning Man Festival rules. Many Vampires of Our Clan find this movement extremely inspiring and find themselves right at home when they attend. Millionaires and artists come together in a variety of social outlets with a diverse group of individuals supporting them as an audience.

Chivalry

Vampire Chivalry is to embrace both real life and the realistic elements of historical chivalrous behavior, and to honor long-standing traditions of civility, courtesy and honor, courtly love, personal nobility and elegance. This remains a perfect expression of the Black Veils.

Historically, chivalry was related to knighthood in the middle ages, focused on service to others and originated in military training. Johan Huizinga wrote several chapters in his book "The Waning of the Middle Ages" about chivalry and how it affected the lives of those in the middle ages. He stated that chivalry is "pride aspiring to beauty, and formalized pride gives rise to a conception of honor, which is the pole of noble life."

When exploring the concepts of chivalry historically in medieval literature, main elements of chivalry include duty to other countrymen, mercy, courage or valor, fairness and a promise to protect the weak, duty to god, being faithful, obedience to Virtue, and of course duty to ladies (the most common aspect of chivalry), treating them with gentleness and grace.

For the Sabretooths, chivalries have been modernized and are a set of inspirations on how to honor other Vampires and how to behave in the mundane world, for a chivalrous Vampire is a powerful individual indeed. Historical examples of knights include William Marshal, Godfrey of Bouillon and Bertrand du Geoselin.

Civility

The concept of Civility and Vampires goes hand-in-hand with basic Vampire Courtesy in modern times. Civility in its most basic form is about habits of personal living which empower the community. As a Black Veil, Vampire class comes down to basic common sense. Civility is to first act like ladies and gentlemen, even as a highly individualistic Vampires, and remain civil and courteous to each other.

Trying to avoid foul language while at the same time being diplomatic when resolving disputes, decent manners, courteous behavior and class are all related to the concept of Vampire Civility. The Sabretooth Vampire in order to be considered evolved has to act as such, so they are more empowered through their behavior.

Vampire Civility is something which is expected of all those who are a part of the Clan and the culture which surrounds it. No matter how solitary or individualistic modern Vampires are, it is expected that they maintain a high level of class and Civility when interacting in the mundane world, be it for business, socializing or casual interactions.

Courtesy

ampire Courtesy is a fundamental Black Veil that comes from the concept of the courtly manners expected of aristocracy from ancient to modern times. Many Vampires are courtiers who embrace a level of etiquette and decorum that is encouraged in the Black Veils.

Courteous behavior is a skill, and exhibits a sense of sophistication involving not only etiquette, but also good conversation and intellectual prowess. Examples of Vampire Courtesy that are part of Black Veils include Aesthetics, Chivalry, Elegance, Gifting, Greeting, Hospitality, and Seduction.

Many Vampires also consider the concept of courting through seduction as part of the slow and proper process of attracting a potential lover, business associate, or friend. Each court, house, and tribe within the Vampire Culture will have their own etiquette. It is important to do your best to be educated on their "house customs" to be a good host and or excellent guest.

Craftsmanship

Vampires are creators and the Black Veil of Craftsmanship is a virtue which describes the Vampire's love for original and hand made crafts including custom fangs, unique jewelry, masks, couture clothing, paintings, airbrushing, tattoos and the like.

Members of the Sabretooth Family share an appreciation of things original, spiritual and non-manufactured. This valuation mainly comes from the reality that the community and clan were built upon fangs that had to be hand made. Vampires also love to support each other and encourage creativity; this is an element of the Vampire Culture that is very strong.

NOTICE: Its VERY important to obtain a proper license to use the Legacy Ankh by getting a proper PHOENIX WARRANT from the Sabretooth Clan. Those with this license can use the Vampire Legacy Ankh officially for their various projects. No one is permitted to use the Legacy Ankh for commercial purposes without this endorsement. Examples of those with Phoenix Warrants include Airship Isabella and Alchemy Gothic Ltd.

Culture

Vampires, no matter their background, are drawn to an excellence in tastes. This can be expressed through such rich avenues as arts, history, museums, theatre, humanities, high culture, couture, quality food, languages, traditions and etiquette. This comes from an insatiable lust for life and all of the elements within it.

The very word "culture" hails from the Latin **cultura** and originates from **colere**, which means "to cultivate." This is exactly what Vampires do, with a love of patterns integrated into the social meanings and symbolic thoughts which humanity has the capacity to bring to life.

On the next level there is "Vampire Culture," which is a shared set of attitudes, values, goals, and practices that characterize the philosophy of Vampires. These very Black Veils are both elementary and defining descriptions of the Vampire Culture of traditions and concepts that have cumulated since the modern "Vampire Age" which began in the early 1990s.

Dance

For beings that hold Elegance as a Virtue, Dance is the ultimate spiritual experience and a form of meditation in motion. The human form that the Vampire inhabits is a refined and beautiful machine, with movement of all types being forms of expression, communication and art.

Dance is a major Black Veil and often associated with the Kitra / Pulse energy of the Current. Many Vampires are belly dancers and burlesque performers, like the Vampire Muse Jeniviva (1975-2011 RIP).

Vampires often find Dance is one of their most important forms of release, be it dancing at a local gothic club, going to a rave, or seeing a ballet or modern dance performance. There is no limit to the forms of Dance embraces by Vampires.

Vampire havens and Balls often have tribal and experimental belly dancing as a centerpiece of the event, with performances contributing to the ritual of the communal dance floor. There are now an upcoming generation of Vampire choreographers who organize performances amongst members of the Family.

Dayside

The Dayside is the objective reality of the mundane and profane world as experienced by the five senses. Here science, rationality, reason, and logic are the prime rule. In the Black Veils, to have a strong foundation in the Dayside one must master several global life dynamics, including focus on the Self, Creativity, Glamour (a part of Lesser Magic), Wellness, Solvency, Preservation, and Perpetuity.

Such dynamics cover the fundamental basics of mundane life such as making money, handling taxes, physical and psychological health, social skills, street smarts, personal financial management, and so on. The ultimate goal of the Dayside is to focus on the optimal mastery of this "Mortal Coil" (the incarnation or life from conception to death). When referring to the "Dayside Family", the Black Veils perspective is a reference to a biological birth / blood family.

Decadence

he Vampire is Decadent; a luxurious life is well within the grasp of the Black Veil Vampire. However, Vampires are no fools and live within their means in order to balance their own equilibrium. Decadence is projected through obtaining and enjoying the pleasures of life that can be obtained realistically. Instead of going to an overpriced expensive restaurant, the Vampire might cook an exquisite dinner for a tenth of the price and find a beautiful riverside location in which to seduce their date for a unique full moon picnic.

Spoiling lovers, enjoying beautiful things, relishing amazing foods and embracing the realities of beauty all come from the heart and spirit of the Vampire vs. the wallet. It is possible to enjoy life without being rich monetarily. The Vampire refuses to give in to societal pressure or advertising that states otherwise.

Draconian

raco was a politician in the 7th century BC who laid down the first set of laws in the city state of Athens. He was known for his harshness, and the term "Draconian" was eventually coined to mean extreme inflexibility. The Draconian Veil is one which is rarely seen, but if put into a certain position, the Black Veil Vampire might have to employ this Veil.

Vampire philosophy adopts a full Draconian perspective temporarily as a result of an emergency and looking at the reality of life. Look to examples from Friedrich Wilhelm Nietzsche and the idea of Social Darwinism for more information on this concept.

Only in rare circumstances does one want to see the Draconian side of a Vampire which is harsh, aggressive, intelligent, predatory, and sharp. Vampires will often band together when employing this Black Veil in protection of the Clan or their individual interests. However in most circumstances the Draconian Black Veil is toned down and only used in a light sense to acknowledge the reality that survival in human society is not always a walk in the park.

Dragon

or the Vampire and mundane alike the Dragon represents Mystery, Power, Immortality, Divinity, Creation, Ascension, Spiritual Enlightenment, Flight, Wealth, and Creation of life through fire. The Dragon Veil draws upon the mythological and spiritual legends in culture that represent this Spirit and are deeply ingrained in the legends of Vampires.

In Romanian mythology the word Dracul represented not only the word for Dragon, but also was synonymous with demons, vampires, and the fabled "Order of the Dragon" with member Vlad Tepesh (Vlad III, Prince of Wallachia), who was the basis for the historical character Dracula.

Many consider the Dragon to be representative of the deepest elements of Our primal, embodied within the reptilian brain. The reptilian brain was first identified by Dr. Paul D. MacLean and is the lower part of the brain which controls involuntary functions and shares the same structure as reptiles.

The Dragon stands symbolically and functionally in real life as a strong tool of power for Vampires. Thus many will have Dragon imagery in their lairs and be drawn to the characteristics of Dragon mythology and symbolism itself.

Drama

There are two types of drama in the Vampire World according to the Black Veils: theatrical drama (the good kind) and melodrama (the negative kind). It is essential to be able to identify the difference between these two types of drama and to know how to manage both..

"THEATRICAL DRAMA" is wearing fangs, costumes, roleplaying, acting and generally knowing the difference between fantasy and reality. Theatrical drama can be done through being in character or on stage and is the providence of Greek tragedy and comedy. Vampire: the Masquerade roleplayers are a fine place for such drama or interacting with others. However everyone involved is aware this is only for fun, the experience and atmosphere, dropping it when the story or event is over. Never succumb to melodrama and try and keep the theatrical drama safe, sane and consensual. Theatrical drama requires immense creativity and education, often acting classes or skill with creating costumes.

"MELODRAMA" is highly negative and is the providence of the "gaja" and "Asari" who psychically drain emotions and creative negative contexts to get attention. This drama is poisonous and harmful to the Vampire World and should be avoided and condemned at all costs. Treating people poorly for no reason or out of jealousy, harping on others and trolling are examples of this type of drama. Obviously it is not only limited to the Vampire World but in every culture, however with the prevalence of emotional psychic vampirism (which is about making this drama) they are drawn to positive energy to take it from others. Such drama pushes the quality and good people out of the Vampire World and makes everyone look bad.

Egregores

Egregores are spontaneously or intentionally created elementals born from the vibe and philosophical ties of a group. They are given life and existence by collective agreement, offerings, and recognition. The word egregore means "watcher" and they were originally elementals created by magical groups to serve as protective guardians. Many "godforms," from one perspective, can be seen as egregores which are jointly created by the divine spirit and fueled by life force given by a god's worshippers. Egregores can be born, evolve, and die or become weakened by being forgotten, as has been the case with many gods and goddesses from ancient history. Even some Catholic Saints are examples of ancient godforms being taken over and evolved into saints in the Catholic pantheon.

In modern times many egregores appear in pop culture. They may be mascots, symbols of political parties, or branded characters like Eddie, the mascot for the rock band Iron Maiden. Characters in films (Tyler Durden from Fight Club and Darth Vader from Star Wars) also have egregores. Superheroes such as Wolverine, Wonder Woman, and Superman are other examples of personified egregores. The fans of these characters become the egregore's worshippers and they make continual offerings to the egregore through the attentions of a devoted fan base.

Modern egregores often are "viral" and evolved by collective social dynamics such as trends without a well-established central creator, like Santa Claus or the Easter Bunny. However, others are created by specific artists, writers, or corporate marketing departments. These creators are equivalent to the egregore's priesthood. The collective actions, agreement, traditions, and culture of an egregore's creators and fans result in the creation of a collective conciousness for the egregore. In today's society comic book readers worship Batman just as surely as the ancient Greeks worshipped Zeus! The best example of a character having a modern egregore is none other than C'thulhu, the Deep One from H.P. Lovecraft's novels.

Elders

Elders within the Sabretooth Clan are those who have had their fangs for 5 years or more and are known as "Purple Stones." They are considered "Elders." However the meaning of an elder in its truest sense is an individual who is wise, teaches and guides the younger members of a community.

The title Elder is an honorific. Confusion occurs when people consider it a formal title that carries a great deal of power, when in fact Elder simply means wise - someone who has been around longer than the adolesecent Vampire. Being an Elder does not give power over others, bestow any super powers, or imply Mastery of the vampirism or knowledge of Black Veils. Many Elders stay out of Vampire politics and have simply been around a long time.

True elders have made a significant and tangible contribution to the community. They organize ongoing events, write influential books, are master craftsmen, and host educational courses. This level of mastery usually takes at least five years of active participation in the VC, but is not just putting in the time; having applicable knowledge is essential. Many who claim to be Vampire "Elders" know nothing about Vampire history, lore, culture, magic, energy work, terminology, or any form advanced knowledge. Thus it is important to challenge those who claim to be Elders with an understanding of Vampiric history, culture, philosophy, and knowledge. True Elders don not need to flaunt titles. When you meet one you will recognize their knowledge and see the way they carry themselves.

Outside the Sabretooth Clan there are many definitions of Elderhood. Each clan, coven, and community may have its own definition, but the Vampire World usually follows and is inspired by the Black Veils and the Sabretooth Clan.

Elegance

he Vampires who embraces this Black Veil are the perso-
nification of simple and effective refinement, dignity, and
grace. This Veil, in the Vampire sense, truly came to be in
the 19th and 20th centuries from the modern retellings of
Vampire legends and myths in literature, film, and fiction.

The Vampire's seductive ability is based on their being elegant,
noble, and an honorable predator that acknowledges their animal
nature. Many Vampires, once they begin the steps of transformation
from mortal to immortal perspectives, simplify in their lives. They
slow down, plan and then execute their presentation to the world.
This conserves energy for later use and reduces wasteful actions.

The most obvious expression of Elegance is within their aesthetics,
grooming, attitude, body language and dress. Examples include the
Vampire Gent wearing a simple black on black suit or the Vampire
Witch donning a regal dress that accentuates her best features. Ac-
cessories including discrete Vampiric symbols such as rings or acces-
sories of the Legacy Ankh and Ouroborous. What is most important
is that it is rare for a fully mature Vampire to overdo their appearance
and complicate their Elegance, keeping simplicity as the first prio-
rity.

Thus the Black Veil of Elegance projects throughout the Current of
the Vampire and empowers their other Vampire Virtues such as Glamour, Mystery, Romance, and Seduction.

Elite

Vampires are Elitist. If everything was created equal there would never be anything special or unique, nor would anything evolve. The same goes for life, in both the Vampire and mundane culture. Everyone should have equal opportunity, but there are talents, skills and natural abilities that are learned, inspired and genetic. Vampires are elitist, but not in a malicious way, just in recognition of mundane gifts.

The Vampire concept of Elite is no different than the sense of standards that are maintained at any Ivy League scholastic university. Many will test the deeper Vampire Mysteries, few will find success. For many years We tried to appeal to the lowest common denominator and welcome everyone in the Vampire World and accept all views. This did not work. It prevented focus and created distractions to Xepher.

Now the Sabretooth Clan has regrouped and focuses inwards as a movement. Think of this as the "Renaissance of Our Vampirism," and the Family serves as a think-tank for those individuals to gather, network and exchange ideas.

Emotional Vampires

In traditional esoteric and occult parlance "traditional psychic vampires" are individuals who create negative emotional states in order to "psychically drain" others of their emotional energy. Within the Black Veils, we call these emotional vampires "ASARAI." Two great sources of information about these emotional parasites are Psychic Self Defense by Dion Fortune and The Satanic Bible by Anton Szandor LaVey, especially the chapter "Not all Vampires Drink Blood." Emotional vampires can be found in every walk of life and certainly are not exclusive to the Vampire World. Yet they are very drawn to the positive people in the VC. They can be easily identified by a variety of signs that include constant complaining, a negative attitude, being emotional leeches, creating drama, and making others feel responsible for them. NOTE: in old parlance psychic vampire referred to emotional vampires, however these two terms have become divergent, psychic (energy) and emotional (emotions).

Most often there is nothing metaphysical about emotional vampires and their manipulations are purely emotional and psychological. It is often impossible to reason with emotional vampires as they keep going in circles and usually never admit they are wrong. A perfect example of an emotional vampire is an individual who says negative things about everyone around them, raising drama and focusing all the attention on themself, and becoming hostile if others do not respond. Even organizations and many situations can have the same effects as an "emo-vamp."

Temporary states of emotional psychic vampirism are called sympathetic vampirism. Sympathetic vampirism is similiar to traditional psychic vampirism but it is only temporary. Anyone can end up as a temporary sympathetic vampire due to trauma, physical or mental illness, extraordinary misfortune, or being a victim of an emotional vampire. Emotional vampirism can be healed over time or balanced out through therapy, relaxation, meditation, willpower and positive energy work.

The only way to protect against emotional psychic vampires is to identify and avoid them when possible. If this is impossible, reduce contact with them as much as possible especially a work place or are in your immediate family or social circle. Black Veils Vampirism promotes majestic and empowered beings. The emotional psychic vampire is completely the opposite. In recent years there has been a growing movement of ethical psychic vampires, or individuals who are aware of what they are and seek a solution through energetic training, metaphysical techniques and ethical feeding.

Enterprising

With the Black Veil of Materialism, Dayside and a Love of Life the Vampire must be able to be enterprising in life. Some Vampires naturally embrace this Veil for their own Dayside success, others see it only as a necessity; whatever the purpose, it is the results that matter.

To be enterprising is to be an entrepreneur, which is someone who has a new enterprise, venture or idea and then takes the risks and accountability inherent in the success or failure of the project. Like the old adage says, "The entrepreneur shifts economic resources out of lower and into higher productivity and greater yield."

Enterprise requires leadership, vision and risk taking, yet not foolishness. Often the enterprising Vampire must break the status quo or reinvent it in order to find their niche. They must be creative, determined and a wayseer in their own unique right.

The Vampire Culture is empowered by this Black Veil, seeing bars, clubs, businesses, art galleries, salons, make up, fashion, music, performance groups, mask makers and the like furthering a "Vampire economy" - the foundation of a culture.

Family

What is most surprising to many is that the Vampires highly value the Veil of Family. Sabretooths being tribal, passionate, loving and courteous naturally have a sense of family culture. The Black Veil of Family has always been a strong element and center of the culture of the Sabretooth Clan.

For example, the interactions between two individuals who have had fangs made or are in agreement about the Veils will have a kinship that is unknown to those outside such a bond. Family is something many of us seek. In the 1990s at Long Black Veil, it was very popular to celebrate Mother's Day, where the Vampires would bring their birth mothers and we would celebrate them with a big party - yes free champagne for moms on that day!

Those from outside the community will see us as Goths being rebels and rejecting their birth families. This could not be further from the case, as the Family Veil encourages a strong, loving bond with all members of one's birth family. Yet this is not always so, with most Vampires who are so individualistic that they are often loners and may have decent yet distant relations with their mundane family and use the Clan as their surrogate Nighside Family. Since the founding of the Sabretooth Clan on August 7th 1995 the concept of Family is one of the major Black Veils.

Fangs

Fangs, a primary classic symbol of the Vampire, can be a powerful psychological tool ; getting fanged a rite of passage. Within the Vampire mythos, fangs are representative of many of the Black Veils especially Elegance, Primal, Romance and Seduction.

Fangs represent four primary elements:

1. Fangs are PRIMAL connecting one to their animalistic nature.
2. Fangs are a MASK, psychologically shapeshifting and disconnecting from the mundane.
3. Fangs are a MAGIC TRICK of Glamour (Lesser Magic). They are so realistic they are a tool of illusion. Thus every Vampire is a magician.
4. Fangs are a SEX TOY and enhance the art of seduction by nibbling and the "Fang Fetish."

Fangsmiths (those who make custom fangs) have consistently noticed that when an individual gets their fangs and looks in the mirror for the first time, there is a subtle shift or transformation as they begin to view themselves differently. There is nothing metaphysical about this - it is a psychological metamorphosis.

Fangs should always made by a professional Fangsmith. Special-effects fangs are usually made overly large to create the proper image on camera and most dentists are not trained or skilled in fangsmithing. Your fangs should be small and subtle caps made without a bridge (so you can speak easily), and prepared from the highest-quality dental acrylics.

Good fangs will be customized to your face and tooth color. Unlike the cheap, boxed fangs available in most Halloween shops, will be fitted for you, making you feel that the fangs are part of yourself. Many Vampires wear their fangs often and feel incomplete without them, as fangs are the ultimate symbol of our Vampiric Nature.

Fashion

ampire Fashion is different from individual to individual and comes in a variety of styles. Steampunk aesthetics are very common in the 2000s, however in the 1990s and today many Vampires are drawn to the style akin to those found in the film "The Matrix." Vampire clothing or "Vampire garb" generally comes in three forms: court, chameleon, and ceremonial. In all cases there is often a simplistic elegance and sophistication in the Vampire's presentation of themselves.

One might think that Vampires are all goths. This again is far from the truth, as many have their Dayside image, which is normal but fashionable daily wear with hints of Vampire garb. Those who embrace the Black Veil of the Warrior will often wear ritual clothing or priestly collars and suits. Vampire Gents will often don black on black suits. Vampire Witches will often project their femininity through classy and alluring attire.

For events such as the Endless Night Vampire Ball, "courtly attire" is expected and no expense or effort is spared by the attendees. The styles include steampunk, gothic, medieval and historical garb, masks, Victorian, black tie, cocktail dresses, costumes, top hats, corsets, belly dance attire, fetish, latex, leather etc. However, no true Vampire would ever be caught looking trashy.

Film

One might think that Black Veil Vampires are specifically focused on vampire genre films but this is far from the reality. The number one film embraced by members of the Sabretooth Clan is without a doubt "Fight Club," followed by "The Matrix" trilogy and Stanley Kubrick's classic "Eyes Wide Shut."

However, vampire movies of course remain popular such as Interview with the Vampire, Bram Stoker's Dracula, Queen of the Damned (more the soundtrack than the film itself,) The Lost Boys, Nosferatu, Blade and of course the Underworld series of movies. Other movies include Lord of War, The Dark Crystal, Lord of the Rings, Labyrinth, A Clockwork Orange, 2001: A Space Odyssey, Star Wars or just about any film directed by Stanley Kubrick or Alfred Hitchcock!

Whatever the film, most Sabretooth Vampires love cinema, be it a classic vampire film series or a unique film which aids in the concept of Glamour, Creativity, and the Legacy.

Fledglings

ledglings, also known as "white stones" within the Sabretooth Clan. These are new Vampires who have been introduced to the Vampire lifestyle and clan, recently awakened, and have gone through the Rites of Transformation, which are the first time seeing themselves in the mirror with their fangs on. In the sense of the Clan, these are individuals who are within a year and a day of their first time getting fangs made. In context, fledglings are the "youngsters" of the VC.

One fun thing is the "fledgling lisp," which is the adjustment period while new Vampires learn to speak with fangs. This is a secret rite of passage within the Sabretooth Clan.

Fledglings are often excited and want to jump right into the activities of the Family, bringing new ideas and excitement to the Sabretooth Clan and Vampire Culture. Others watch and wait, keeping their distance to make sure they choose when they become active.

Gentlemen

The Vampire Gentleman is the manner of conducting one-self that all Sabretooth men strive to achieve and embrace along with the Black Veils of Courtesy, Chivalry, Honour, Love and Loyalty. Here are some traits of a quintessential Vampire Gent:

The Gent has MANNERS "a person's outward bearing; way of speaking to and treating others." He knows what good manners are. He holds doors for ladies. He understands the customs of wherever he is to avoid unnecessarily offending someone. Gents shall be at their best in actions and deeds. A Gent never talks about himself too much.

The Gent is CULTURED and able to speak on many subjects, like art, culture, music, cinema, history, and mythology. He should be well-versed in at least a few subjects in order to educate and entertain with conversation.

The Gent is DRESSED WELL. According to magician Dr. Harlen Tarbell creator of "The Tarbell Course in Magic," a magician should be the best dressed, but not over dressed person in the room. For example showing up to a pool party, don't wear a tuxedo nor be sloppy, but stand out by looking good.

The Gent must BE COMFORTABLE. Famed talk show host Jonny Carson who had a line of suits in the 1970's always maintained that, "If you wear the suit, the suit doesn't wear you." A gentleman needs to feel comfortable in his clothing.

The Gent SPEAKS CLEARLY without profanity, and never raises his voice unless absolutely necessary.

CHIVALRY is how to treat a lady or your companion, the dictionary definition is the combination of qualities expected of an ideal knight, especially courage, honor, courtesy, justice, and a readiness to help the weak.

Finally the Gent has DISCRETION. Be private and discrete in all things as people respect discretion.

Gifting

Gifting is a traditional Black Veil that an outsider would never expect from Vampires. This simple act builds on the Veils of Hospitality and Courtesy, and functions to support free will and create connections of energy. Gifting is not about bribery or expecting something in return, but to simply show another individual you honor and appreciate them.

The most common gift within the Black Veil culture is the offering of a fang making session with a Fangsmith for a friend, lover, or companion. However, gifts are often extended in the form of ankhs and copies of this book or "Vampire World History",for those who wish to delve deeper in to the deeper elements of vampiric history.

Custom made and personalized gifts are also very common such as a customized t-shirt, a painting or a piece of art signed by the creator. Over the years as a Fangsmith I have been given some pretty weird gifts from customers but what I find most touching is when they write a letter which comes from their heart and actually mail it. This is a dying art.

In the end, Gifting is a great way to show appreciation and empower the courtesy, hospitality and unity of the Vampire Culture.

Gifts

In The Vampire Chronicles novels by Anne Rice, many Vampires have "gifts"; powers unique to that individual. For example, Lestat read minds, Marius had the ability to cloud human minds, and Claudia had her youth and innocence to aid her in the hunt. Within the Black Veils and Sabretooth Clan, these fictions are parallel in reality, with Vampires are empowering ourselves with these ideas and translating them into real life. We encourage each practicing Vampire to discover and embrace one "power", which will be their Vampire Gift to develop.

Each individual should find their own "dharma", their purpose or passion, and build from there. This is explored in the Rites of Transformation in the Sabretooth Clan. For example Frater Asryen has the passion of knowledge of Paris and is an authority on this subject. Jeniviva's Gift was her passion and talent at performance and belly dance. Victor Magnus's Gift is a thirst for knowledge of military history. Magister Ur's is a talent for writing and spiritual perspectives. Zak Bagans is a great ghost hunter, and Myke Hideous's Vampire Gift is musical talent and performance. Their Vampire Gifts are their passions and help define who they are as individuals and inspire both mundanes and other Vampires alike.

Do you have a dream to be realized? Could it be dance, music, painting, photography, writing, business, charisma, DJing, chess, a sport, skill with tracking or hunting, knowledge on a specific subject, or a supernatural sense of humor? An unexplored ability, talent, or passion which is yet to manifest or already a dream you want to further? This is the nature of the Sabretooth Vampire! Embrace Xepher.

Glamour

he Glamour is apart of Lesser Vampire Magic and represents the mystic powers of mesmerism, seduction, and control that legends and literature assign to the Black Veil Vampire. A "Glamour" may be described as a magic spell, or, most commonly, an alluring or fascinating attraction. The moth that immolates itself within a candle flame is irresistibly drawn to the burning glamour of the fire.

Fledglings and those new to Vampire philosophy are often embroiled in the aesthetics of gothic Vampire imagery, like fangs and dramatic attire. The mundane world loves such trappings, as they are so many eternally seduced by the fantasy of the vampire. Fangs represent a powerful element of the Glamour, yet it is only the beginning and an example in that it is actually a magic trick, thus each Vampire is a magician. People want to believe so much that they are honestly deceived; so many in these modern times need to believe in vampires and we play off this.

Glamour on an advanced level can include actual magic tricks, employment of Neuro Linguistic Programming (NLP) techniques, traditional seduction, aromatherapy, being well dressed and clean cut and a multitude of other concepts. Glamour is a powerful vehicle to move forward in life, be it amongst Vampires or within the mundane world and weaves the Veils of elegance and seduction together into an effective and almost unstoppable Vampire Culture.

Gotham Halo
(new york city)

Gotham Halo is the Sabretooth Clan term for the New York metro area including the 5 boroughs of New York City, Westchester, Northern New Jersey, Long Island, parts of Upstate New York, Southern Connecticut and Rockland County. Many called Gotham the "Rome of Vampires" and had the largest collection of lifestyle vampires, clans, households and courts than any other place on earth. Gotham Halo has a long Vampire history because this is the historical seat where the Sabretooth Clan was founded by Father Sebastiaan on August 7th 1995, initiating Gotham as the first Halo. The first Endless Night Vampire Ball, which took place in February 1996 at the Bank nightclub, officially launched the new era of Gotham, Sabretooth Clan and Vampire Culture.

In the 1990s nightclubs like Limelight (a deconsecrated church at 660 6th Ave 1983-2000), MOTHER (432 Washington St. home of Long Black Veil, Jackie60 and Click + Drag 1996 to 2000) and the Bank (225 E. Houston Street 1990-1999) were the centre of the vampire community and officially recognized havens by the Sabretooth Clan. In March of 1997 Empress Chi Chi Valenti and Father opened Long Black Veil & the Vampyre Lounge at MOTHER. LBV is where the vampire subculture on the East Coast of the USA and first Black Veils and Legacy Ankh were originated. Katherine Ramsland (Anne Rice biographer) wrote Piercing the Darkness (1998) about the 1996 disappearance of investigative journalist Susan Walsh, bringing national attention to the New York Vampire Culture.

A Vampire Halo has an egregore (thought form or energy signature) that is comprised of the history and interactions of Sabretooth Clan and Vampire Culture within this geographic area combined with the mundane culture and energy. Before the term and concept of a Halo was coined in Amsterdam by Crystalfang and Father Sebastiaan in 2004, there existed a monthly meeting called "The Court of Gotham" starting in 1997. The name Gotham takes its name not from the city of Batman legend, but from the fanciful tales of author Washington Irving and his depiction of Dutch colonial era. These fantastic stories included the Headless Horseman (yes Sleepy Hollow is in Gotham Halo) and Rip Van Winkle.

Gourmet

ampires are Gourmets; as many cultures feel that food is life, so does the Black Veil Vampire. With this love of food, the Vampire culture is known for its elaborate dinners, banquets, medieval-style feasts and love of clean, quality food and the ceremonies and traditions, which go with dining on them. Many Black Veil Vampires are lovers of tea, absinthe, mead, and red wine (as you might imagine), often frequenting restuarants, tea salons, wine tastings, or visiting vineyards.

An interesting note is that many Vampires are vegetarians or vegans; seemingly hypocritical from the outside this makes perfect sense for the Vampire who loves life and wishes not to destroy it. Vampires are hunters and do it as a way to see what it takes to keep oneself alive by taking another life; the reality of the jungle. Some Vampires will only eat meat they kill themselves and otherwise live a vegetarian diet, again to remind them of the value of life.

However in the long run, most Vampires love the tradition of cooking food themselves, controlling the contents of what they eat and only obtaining the best quality cuts of meat, vegetables and ingredients.

In the end, life for the Vampire is often centered on food and sharing it with each other. There are few greater pleasures for the Vampire than food.

Greeting

The "Gotham Greeting" is a unique cultural handshake and like the Gotham Vampire Howl it was a tradition created by Master Metal Manipulator D. This is one tradition in a trinity of traditions created within the Clan and brought to the greater Vampire subculture by our beloved maestro.

It usually involves the grasping of hands with the junior initiating the Greeting after patiently waiting in respect. Then after the handshake and often a nod the junior member then leaves a kiss on the back of the senior member's hands, and then the senior member follows suit. Sometimes a hug follows.

The Vampire Greeting is often called a "Lost Tradition" and has been resurrected as of this writing by many within the Clan and Vampire community in Europe and in Gotham.

Halloween

alloween, also known as Samhain (pronounced sow-in) in modern Pagan culture, might be thought of as the most important holiday for Black Veil Vampires. Usually celebrated and observed on the Saturday before or on Halloween proper. This time of year many holidays take place including the Celtic New Year, the Mexican Day of the Dead and All Saints Day. These three days of festivities are often considered the most popular time of the year for all Vampires, both Sabretooth and non-Sabretooth. These are the nights of balance and metamorphosis, as well as the Vampire New Year inspired by the Celtic/Pagan New Year.

Halloween night also marks the time when the Barrier Between Worlds, the physical and spiritual, is at its thinnest, with some vampires using this time to pursue deeper into Vampire Mysteries and spiritual endeavors.

Halloween is a gateway leading to the longer nights of the year during the end of Harvest. New Orleans serves as the centerpiece for Halloween for the Vampires World. This is the largest Vampire gathering in the world. During this festival, we often enjoy expressing our Glamour in full force and walking openly amongst the mundane. Halloween is one of the most open of all celebrations, since Vampires feel they can be more open and free at this time of year.

Halos

he "Halo" is the Black Veil name for major geographic areas, which are sacred to the Sabretooth Family. Specific cities have always been considered Halos and contain large populations of Vampires. The most notable Halos are **Gotham** (New York City), **Angel** (Los Angeles), **Morta** (New Orleans), **Albion** (London), and **Lutetia** (Paris, France).

Each Halo has its own energy signature, personality, history and culture. Halos are exclusively a Black Veil and Sabretooth Clan term and only officially acknowledged when recognized by the Clan itself, often with performing a consecration rite by an officially-ordained Vampire Priest/ess of the Family and Black Veils.

The communities of Vampires and other Awakened live within Halos, they evolve, grow, or diminish according to the collective social interests of the Family. Gotham Halo, often called the "Rome of Vampires," is the largest and most famous of the Halos. It is not restricted by geographic or civic boundaries and so includes the five boroughs of Manhattan, Brooklyn, Queens, The Bronx and Staten Island.

Happiness

Vampires, believe it or not, strive for happiness and contentment in life as a strong Black Veil. Most cultures and religions strive for the ultimate goal of eternal happiness. As each have their own approaches and techniques, so does Vampirism.

Happiness is a state of mental well-being defined by a series of positive emotional states including intense joy and contentment free from suffering. This can be defined in a multitude of ways from religious, psychological, biological and philosophical perspectives. Modern secular culture has defined a concept of positive psychology which employs scientific methods to create such a state.

For the Vampire thinking positive is essential, realizing life is not always fair, that each challenge and obstacle only allows development of an individual who better appreciates moments of contentment. Living a decent, honorable life with respect and dignity are central elements of Vampire Happiness.

Hospitality

As beings of love and passion, Black Veil Vampires are often extremely hospitable, only refraining from entering someone's home unless specifically invited, not out of a curse or some supernatural limitation, but out of respect and courtesy. The Vampire who embraces this Veil shows hospitality to others of the Clan and Family. Even when barely knowing each other, those touched by the Current will often welcome those who would be complete strangers into their home just by knowing that they are Family.

Thus the Vampire can be free to travel the world if they embrace this Black Veil in its fullest and become embroiled in deep personal relationships with others of the Family by a deep connection of the Current. Also true is that the Vampire acts as a proper and courteous guest.

The Hospitality Black Veil also seeks not to impose on another when they have obligations such as work, mundane family or other commitments and never to overstay on their host's hospitality. Being good guests and good hosts reflects a sense of honor and in the days of the internet, restoring a long lost tradition of getting to know each other first and foremost in person.

Houses (Covens)

Household is the most common VC term for a coven of Vampires. These groups were most active from the mid to late 1990s to early 2000s. The term was brought into the VC in 1996 when the Sabretooth Clan adopted it from the Society for Creative Anacronism (SCA) for the Sanguinarium network. Houses serve as circles of people focused on learning, initiation, spiritual development, ritual groups, and socialization. Each house had its own culture, specific philosophy, and more. Some houses were centered around a specific theme like worshipping the goddess Isis or emulating Geisha, while another might be focused on being Viking warriors. The term Houses was chosen to reflect European aristocratic lineages, like the "House of Bourbon," the "House of Windsor," "House of Orange" or the "House of Hapsburg."

Traditionally, Houses operated like pagan covens, were lead by an Elder who took on a leadership position as the Patriarch or Matriarch, the equivalent of a High Priest/ess in a pagan coven. These elder leaders served as the parent, leader, priest, and teacher. New households were often created when existing households reached 13 members. At that point the household split and a new embryonic house known as a "clutch" would form. Within Sabretooth Clan and Sanguinarium, an elder needed a "charter"(official endorsement by the Clan) to officially be recognized. As the new group evolved and organized it would eventually gain the status of household.

In summer of 2005, Sabretooth Clan officially disbanded all the houses within the Clan and established the "Great Houses", better known as the "Pulses" of Kitra (Lovers), Mradu (Warriors) and Ramkht (Magicians). Sabretooth houses wishing to continue simply went independent, yet many still honor their lineage in the Sabretooth Clan Legacy. With the growth of the internet, groups on social media, and public awareness of Vampires, new houses are increasingly less common due to the independent and "ronin" nature of Vampires.

Howl

owling is a tradition kept alive amongst many in many underground Vampire events and at worldwide Endless Night Vampire Ball events during the Cirque. The tradition involves howling like a wolf, which in nature is used to sound an alarm, assemble a pack, or to communicate over great distances.

The Vampire Howl is led by the Master or Mistress of Ceremonies or Impresario during the apex of an Endless Night event or group settings, either to mourn a fallen friend or to celebrate a success.

The originator of the "Gotham Howl" is Master Metal Manipulator D, the designer of the Vampire Legacy Ankh. Within the Black Veils and Sabretooth Clan, the Howl has two functions: first to release the primal "Inner Beast," and to bring people together in chorus and empower the Current.

Humor

Vampires who follow the Black Veils and the Sabretooth Clan often have a good sense of humor. Nothing represents the Vampire's spark of life more than a good laugh. Humor is a truly important Black Veil; being able to laugh at oneself is a power which is symbolic of the Black Veil of the Mirror. The patron spirit of the Endless Night, Fred Samedi and his Acolytes are known to embrace this Veil in its fullness.

It is well known that laughter and humor increase vitality, health and good spirit, thus the Vampire seeking out the secrets of immortality endeavors to laugh more. What would immortality be if everything was taken so seriously?

Vampires also love everything from sarcasm and slapstick to satirical humor, often enjoying TV shows like True Blood (which are humorous and serious at the same time). In the end taking oneself too seriously simply is unhealthy and unbalanced; this the Current knows all too well.

Immortality

ampires love and have a passion for life on such a level that this Black Veil represents the quest to conquer death and live beyond the normal limitations of the human lifespan. How is this possible? Aren't there questions about the ethics of overpopulation, aging, disease or how this is not "natural?" The Black Veil Vampire sees the opposite, they think from a perspective of Self-Preservation with a love for life. They seek to enjoy the benefits of longevity and vitality which modern and future science has begun to unlock in ways never imagined before or even thought to be possible.

Unlocking the secrets of Immortality is to look not just to longevity but also to vitality in health and spirit as we age. It is said by many researchers that people in their 60s are more content and happy than at any other point in their lives. Physical immortality is not currently available as of this writing, but transhumanism, the system of evolving beyond human limits through biotechnologies, nanotechnology, life extension, bionics and merging with machines increases the potential for immortality with every advancement made.

Currently, steps to longevity and vitality include reducing risks to personal life, quitting smoking, increasing health through a well thought out exercise plan, sports, a quality diet and education on life extension technologies. Many Vampires see aging as a disease that is to be cured. Visionary immortalists such as Aubrey De Grey from the UK, organizations such as the Life Extension Foundation and the Immortalist Society are at the forefront of bringing the vision of immortality into reality. Of course simply living in a healthy way with drugs and alcohol in moderation teamed up with a good regimen of quality food and exercise can go a long way in increasing vitality and life extension. The Veil of Immortality is in league with these visions.

Individualist

---

he Vampire's Individuality is deeply rooted in the fact we all make the conscious decision to get our fangs made and sit there, while the Fangsmith gently molds our teeth, either in private or not. The individualism is that we decided and volunteered for this experience.

This is the foundation of Vampire Individualism. Simply put, Vampires are like cats, they cannot be herded or told what to do, and they must be inspired and make the decision based upon their own personal interests.

We are amongst the chosen few; it is by our own choice we are able to wear a mask that is at once a sex toy, a theatrical piece, a magic trick, and an illusion.

Inspiration

ampire legends speak of the hypnotic power of the Vampire's gaze and in a psychological sense there may be some truth behind this legend. This truth comes from Vampires often being sources of inspiration, especially in the artistic sense.

We are often the whisperers in the ears of artists, musicians, dancers, creative individuals, or we are the voice of the "Devil's Advocate" suggesting innovative new ideas, concepts and processes of thinking which come from a surprising source, the Current.

Denying being one who inspires or affects others is to deny the Current. The Family has access to a collective knowledge and experiences in such an intimate diversity, as well as direct knowledge and ideas. Sitting in a fangsmithing booth in a Halloween store over the years, for me, resulted in a personal flow of ideas between highly interesting individuals.

Due to the diversity of the Family, ideas, concepts and visions flow on an international level. So it is not as much about a mystical experience, but a unique shared experience. More authors, artists, dancers, performers and musicians than you think have been able to use the Sabretooth internal network and the Clan as a tool of inspiration, generating a flow of ideas globally. Also those who see our traditions touch them and are influenced by them, surprised to see our uniquely positive views on life and thus become inspired.

khemet
(ancient egypt)

Ancient Egypt was called Khem or "The Black Land" because of the fertile dark soil along the shores of the Nile River. The Nile River valley was part of the Fertile Crescent and one of the places where humankind began. Ancient Egypt is commonly associated with vampires due to the Egyptians' obsession with Immortality. The link between vampires and Ancient Egypt was popularized by Anne Rice in The Queen of the Damned through her fictional characters Queen Akasha and Enkil. There is a reality behind the myths of vampire-like entities in Ancient Egypt. The Egyptians wrote entire manuals about Immortality, such as the Pert em Hru, which means "The Book of Coming Forth by Day." It is known today as the Egyptian Book of the Dead.

In the religion of Khem there were many different parts of the soul. The KA was the equivalent of the soul and the BA was the equivalent of the mind and personality. The Egyptians believed that when the physical body died it must be preserved in order to create a vessel for the Ka and allow the Ba to leave the body, join together and ascend to judgment. The rich would have a Ka shrine attached to their tomb and a priest would feed the Ka spirit offerings of food and substance, as well as performing rituals offering the Ka and lifeforce. If a Ka spirit was not fed properly, it were said to leave its grave and become a Khu, or "luminous one," and feed upon the life force of the living.

The gods and goddesses openly ruled in Khem. The Pharaohs were their incarnations and avatars in the temporal world. Some Vampire legends often recognize the Pharaohs of Khem as vampire like entities; the entire human population willingly offered their lifeforce to their rulers. The time of this "Open Rule" ended in the Christian era when the contemporary economy could no longer sustain the rigorous care of the dead. However, traces of the time of Open Rule survived in traditions such as the belief in the divine right of kings in Europe in the Sangraal legends.

Knight

he Vampire Knight is dedicated to the Black Veils of Gents, Mradu, Chivalry, Warrior, Loyalty, Romance, Honor, Passion and Culture through embracing personal Nobility.

When interacting amongst themselves Vampire Knights often fraternal and stand together. The Knight does not simply go out and declare themself as such, this Black Veil must be lived through action, example and upholding other related Black Veils. The Knight is a provider and lover, romantic and protector. They have no fear of powerful, successful individuals, inspiring others and treating them with respect and dignity.

Although originally for those of masculine persuasions the Vampire Knight is a tradition of fraternity dedicated to becoming better individuals and improving the the Current in themselves. Today many Vampire Ladies and Witches have taken up the Black Veil of the Vampire Knight. They practice modernized chivalry and courtesy, and enjoy in such pursuits as the game of chess, history museums, practicing martial arts, enjoying classic arts of culture, music and dance and priding themselves on being role models for other Vampires.

The Vampire Knight continues the old traditions of cultural empowerment of chivalry in a revised modernized format for the new era.

lairs

he Lair is the personal sanctuary of a Living Vampire. This can be an entire apartment, house or room if they share a dwelling and usually deeply representative of their unique personality. Maintaining a Lair is essential for a Vampire as this is their personal sanctuary. Even if they are in a deep long-term monogamous relationship, each Vampire needs their own space more than the average human.

Lairs are also humorously called "personal sanctums" and as a pun on MTV's cribs they are called "crypts" (yes, some people tried to start a reality show about Vampyre Lairs). Even though each Vampire Lair is different, decor and materials symbolic of the Vampire Lifestyle are often in common.

Often it will be protected from sunlight as many Vampires love to sleep in and the Lair will be decked out to reflect the personality of the owner. Classy and classic baroque furniture is all the rage amongst the Clan these days. Cliché paraphernalia is not uncommon and if used is still displayed with a sense of humor such as coffin tables, antique frames symbolic of mirrors and the colors of red, silver, black, white, yellow, scarlet, crimson and purple often decorate the homes.

Whatever the result, the Vampire's Lair is a private domain and those who embrace this Black Veil truly have the need for a private and secure retreat, which alternatively can be used to entertain guests.

libertine

The Romantic, sensual and immortal minded, the Vampire feels free of mundanes burdens thus has the nature of the true libertine. The average mundane might have the first impression of the Vampire Libertine as a senseless hedonist, but the True Libertine will be true to their sexual nature while respecting the free will of others.

Being individuals with open minds, Vampires are often libertines. But the French term meaning "to be free" doesn't just refer to sexuality. What might be a fetish to an average person is completely normal for Vampires: many of us think fangs are great sensual tools!

Many mortal-minded individuals lie to themselves and deny themselves for the sake of morality; however the Vampire seeks to be completely honest with their nature. Free of lies and social conditionings the Black Veil Vampire embraces who they are be it gay, straight, asexual, fetishistic, transsexual, polyamorous, monogamous, and so on. Yes, even a monogamous individual can be sexually free if they are honest with themselves.

This is by no means an excuse to be senseless hedonists, as the Libertine is direct, honest and true to themselves about their nature and those who they engage with. Yet always does it with class, elegance, personal nobility and respect.

Legacy

he Legacy in the Black Veils is the reference to the story and history of the Sabretooth Clan we all share. The Current and Endless Night events. After Bram Stoker's Dracula, Anne Rice's Vampire Chronicles and Vampire: the Masquerade, the Sabretooth Clan is is greatest influencer on the Vampire Culture. The Legacy is also the immortality that we share with each other. The Second Death in ancient Egypt was when the name and identity of an individual was forgotten. Weaving a Legacy together aids one in achieving and participating in this collective, thus leaving your mark on the world. So contribute, create, find your gifts and support the Legacy.

Individuals' level of connection depends on the contact and involvement they have with the Legacy and the Current. Some have gotten their fangs, attended an event and left. Others have become heavily involved in the Legacy for a lifetime. These are the "flame", and others are casual fans who enjoy their experience but live their dayside lives very separately. Sadly, there are those who become "discordants", who have gone against the flow of the Current and obstruct its flow and will, intentionally or unintentionally.

The Legacy began in the 1990s and has a "prelude" with everything leading up to it in Sabretooth History. Together all of the interactions of the Sabretooths, attendees of Endless Night, our Black Swans, employees and fans each contribute to the story of the Legacy.

life

Vampire just don't survive, they LIVE! One Vampire joked that it was funny how to live is "evil" backwards. Vampires love life, they thrive on experience, creation and having a deep primal thirst for life and seek its continuance.

Call it chi, ki, prana, lifeforce or simply vital energy; an abundance and lust for such energy is extremely important amongst the Immortals. What is most important is the love of life and to enjoy all its beauty, to celebrate the positive and learn from the negative.

Life is a one shot deal from the Dayside perspective of the Black Veil Vampire, so make the most of it. The whining, complaining vampire character Louis of Anne Rice's books hates life and he is depressed. The Vampire is the opposite of this and embraces with honor and pride what they are, reveling in life, enjoying each and every moment as if it were the last. Plan for eternity: live as if it is your last day and celebrate the gift you have been given to be what and who you are.

love

Some say only love can defeat death. Love is an evolved state of the survival instinct to keep relationships together and strong. Overall love is an expression of kindness, affection and compassion.

The Vampire is a creature of love. For the Vampire every love is a different experience. Some examples include romantic love, love of life, fraternal love, parental love, love between Vampires, love of the Self and spiritual love.

English has limited love to one word; however "Vampire Eyes" allows the Vampire to see more of the potential in all living things. Thus first and foremost, the Vampire loves life. More than any time in history, mankind has been seduced by the Vampire Archetype because Vampires are passionate and in love with the Black Veils.

loyalty

he Black Veil of Loyalty is a bond of spirit and mind. The Vampire is raised in human society, yet is alien to the world around them due to those traits of spirit and mind.. The difference is a bond: a form of Loyalty of perception.

For the Vampire, Loyalty is a form of deep-rooted Love. The two are nearly identical, as Love is within Loyalty and Loyalty is within Love. What most unites the Vampires of the Legacy and Sabretooth Clan is, first and foremost, a common experience to remember for a lifetime: their fanging. This experience may happen by stumbling upon a Fangsmith when walking into a Halloween shop, or by a much-anticipated appointment for their fangsmithing session.

The experience of sitting in the fang chair (throne), the anticipation, the laughter, the hazing, and the weird sensations of the first time an individual gets their fangs, is one that no one forgets. The awakening to the Current usually starts with curiosity about Vampires, with the Rites of Transformation following as a major catalyst. This common experience has been called the "Fight Club Effect", with fang clients being akin to members of the fictional Project Mayhem from the Fight Club novel and film.

Machiavellian

Vampires, when they need to be, can without hesitation be considered cunning and employ duplicity in life. This definition is actually close to the definition of Machiavellianism in the Oxford English Dictionary; based on "The Prince," a legendary book by the writer and Renaissance statesman Niccolò Machiavelli from Florence, Italy in the 16th century.

The Black Veil of Nobility encourages mastery of one's own personal kingdom and one's personal space. Thus as an example of noble empowerment, The Prince is an excellent source of inspiration for those wishing to employ the Machiavellian Black Veil.

From the perspective of this Black Veil the Machiavellian Vampire learns from the pages of The Prince examples of power, ruler-ship, leadership, cunning and statesmanship that are required to rule. However this is not about ruling others, but how one Vampire can rule themselves and to navigate life with a sense of mastery in business and personal affairs.

Magic(k)

Within the Sabretooth Clan "Vampire Magic" is a mental and psychological technology of symbols, techniques and systems. Such magic is divided into HIGH (Subjective) and LESSER (Objective) magic. HIGH VAMPIRE MAGIC uses theatrical rituals and ceremonies to create psychodrama to focus emotional energy towards a specific purpose or goal of entering the Nightside. LESSER VAMPIRE MAGIC is "Glamour" through social dynamics and sleight of hand, manipulation, seduction of an individual, group or situation. Vampire magic uses the imagery, romantic, primal, mysterious, aesthetic, seductive, theatrical and empowering elements of the Vampire Mythos.

Ritual, rites and, ceremony are fascinating to many, yet rites of passage, ordeals, and initiatory practices in many traditional forms are lost to modern society. Examples include: coming of age, marriages, funerals, and holiday celebrations. The acquiring of fangs, as part of the "Rites of Transformation" performed on every new Sabretooth, is an initiation and a rite of passage into a new Vampire World. This book is intended to revive these rites within modern culture and reinforce the traditions of the Sabretooth Clan.

Some fundamental elements of Vampire Magic within the Black Veils of the Sabretooth Clan are that it is not completely based on the metaphysical, but "extraordinary" effects and remain within the realm of science, the natural world, and psychology. Vampire magic does not relate to the concepts of either white or black magic, as these are mundane concepts of morality. What defines the purpose of Vampire Magic is the Intent and Will of the Vampire to obtain specific results. True Vampiric ethics do not involve animal or human sacrifice, or harming others physically or mentally. Nor do they advocate worshiping anything but the ego and focus Willpower and mental energy. The goals and aims of Vampire Magic should be attainable and realistic, and magic should not be complex, but simple and spontaneous

Marriage
"blood & roses"

Vampire Marriage within the Black Veils and Sabretooth Clan is also known as "Blood & Roses." This is usually presided by an ordained Priest /ess of the Black Veils. The Vampire marriage is traditionally not legally binding on the first steps. Vampires are encouraged to have two weddings, one Dayside and one Nightside. This is similar to the old northern European tradition of handfasting, now practiced commonly in the neo-pagan world, which is an old form of Celtic marriage. Literally it means to make a contract of marriage. In Old Norse it means to "make a bargain with the hands."

Blood and Roses are conducted on three levels, entitled the "Rings," based on ring exchange:

FIRST RINGS is more of an "engagement" and lasts a year and a day, which can either be renewed, allowed to expire or the couple can move to the second ring.

SECOND RINGS is a marriage that lasts seven years, and like the first it can expire, evolve or be renewed. This is traditionally a legal marriage.

THIRD RINGS is to last for eternity and last beyond death. Metaphysically the souls are bound together to meet again in the next life.

Unlike mundane weddings, the couple makes vows and presides the wedding themselves, while the Priest/ess is in charge of organizing the wedding and functioning as a witness. Vampires are also known to "marry themselves" which is a tradition of proclaiming one is very independent. Vampires rarely get divorced, since the first two levels of marriage have expiration dates and mundane marriage is the leading cause of divorce.

Masks

Throughout history masks have been used in masquerade balls, the Venetian carnival, tribal shamanistic practices, performances, ceremonies and Halloween.

Masks add mystery and anonymity, allowing a rare sense of freedom which lets one bring out aspects of their personality that are not commonly explored. In New York City masquerade balls were made illegal in the 19th century because of events similar to those in the Stanley Kubrick film "Eyes Wide Shut." In Venice, Napoleon outlawed Carnival because of the wild events that surrounded the masked events.

Vampires will often collect masques and use them in many very interesting ways. The Endless Night Vampire Ball events highly encourage masques, but do not require them. This allows the historical and practical sense of freedom to come along with the protection of one's identity and allows media into the events for promotional reasons. Masks are often used in the Red Mass and other ceremonies to create a mental psychodrama to allow the wearer to enter another state of experience.

Mastery

ampire Mastery according to the Black Veils is not about mastering others; it is about mastery of a subject, trade, craft, niche or having mastery in life. The goal is personal greatness. Example masters within history include Benjamin Franklin, DaVinci, Mozart, Einstein, Henry Ford and Darwin. Each of these individuals discovered their own purpose in life and fulfilled it with the utmost success.

According to Robert Greene's book Mastery, there are three levels to achieve mastery: Student, Practitioner, and Master.

STUDENTS: begin exploring the fundamental rules aspects of a specific subject. Here you will "show up, shut up, and take notes." It is essential to focus on a mentor. It is ok to make mistakes here. They are learning the ropes. Within the Vampire community students are commonly known as Initiates, Fledglings, Neophytes, and Dedicants.

PRACTITIONERS: have become adept in their creativity and active application and may make fewer mistakes but generally have an adept grasp on the subject. The practitioner sees the big picture and is free to develop his/her own bigger picture, unique style, and ways of execution. Within the Vampire Culture practitioners are commonly known as Adepts, Calmac, Sorors or Fraters.

MASTERS: are called such after an estimated 10,000 hours or 5 years actively pursuing a subject or craft. This takes time and recognition only comes through true achievement. Within the Vampire Culture masters are commonly known as Elders or Magisters.

Many Vampires pursue and seek "Mastery" of the Black Veils by memorizing and being familiar with all of the teachings and terminology within and apply them within their lives. They are often seen as the most valued of individuals within the Family due to their knowledge, wisdom and how to apply those through personally setting an example.

Materialistic

The Black Veil Vampire is not only spiritual and magical but is equally materialistic through embracing this Black Veil i.e. "know the value of a dollar." However, "currency" as it is humorously called is an energy, which is required to make things happen. There is no greater force on this planet to the mundane and they would betray even their very own gods over money.

What makes this Black Veil so important is that Vampires see money as a tool, a vehicle to get plane tickets, pay rent or a mortgage, feed one's family or a multitude of other uses. Many underground cultures (until the financial crisis of the late 00s) scoffed at the concept of showing or possessing wealth. This does not stop the Vampire from desiring luxury items, its just they seek sensible and reasonable ways to obtain such things.

However the Vampire does not flaunt or throw money around to show off, through simple elegance they love hand made artifacts over manufactured items and know the value of hard work. For this Black Veil is not about senseless materialism, it is about elegance and simplicity to get what one needs to enjoy the beauty of life.

The Vampire seeks financial responsibility and freedoms, to be responsible for oneself and to not burden others or to ask for handouts. The Vampire materialist is dedicated to self-sufficiency and independence from external help. The Vampire that embraces this Dayside foundation sees the liberation in having a strong financial foundation.

Mirrors

Vampires love to look at themselves in the Mirror, of course for the purposes of learning about the Self and to fulfill a narcissistic self-love. In reality the mirror is one of the three symbols of the Vampire, especially ones with a black surface, which are known as speculums. There are many legends and superstitions about how mirrors can reflect the soul, be used to see into the astral (spirit world), and ability to see into one's own eyes to identify the Higher Self.

Most commonly known is the superstition that vampires cast no reflection in the mirror because they have no soul. However in reality Vampires have the same physical bodies as anyone else and in the Dayside perspective obviously cast a real reflection. In many magickal traditions such as witchcraft, mirrors are used for scrying and divination.

From a Dayside perspective Vampires see mirrors as a way of self reflection; one example is the ceremony known as the "taste of eternity" or "throning" in which one looks directly into one's own eyes. With this exercise the concepts of time and space will fall away and one will be able to experience their primal self.

Moots

The Black Veil tradition of moots differs from other events in that they function as social events, yet are informal. Examples of Moots include planned meet and greets, discussions over dinner or coffee, or after parties following a formal Vampire Ball. Gatherings such as these are perfect places to make in-person contact with others of the Family. Unlike formal and private Family gatherings such as Salons and Courts, Moots can be held in more exposed public places such as restaurants, taverns, cocktail lounges, coffee shops, or parks.

Moots should not be held in loud bars or during nightclub events, as a sense of intimacy is essential to the meeting. If possible, organize a moot in a classy and fabulous location that will add to the experience such as a nice restaurant near a canal or a beautiful park or in a unique restaurant that has an amazing theme. Tops of buildings with a restaurant such as in the Eiffel Tower or the lobby of a 4 star hotel are good examples. Always look good for such events as to represent the Family.

Moots are a time-honored Vampire tradition and are meant to encourage glamour and the Black Veils. Always remember to dress well, be confident, and project the Black Veils with pride and strength!

Mundane

undanes are people who are "Laymen" to the Black Veils and Vampire subculture. We often call them jokingly "Muggles." They are the normal people who are unfamiliar our ways and or have not been exposed to our culture. It is rather interesting that with the release of the "Lord of the Rings" movies and the popularity of "Twilight" and the television series "True Blood," the mundane world has become more and more curious and even seduced by our Glamour.

The term mundane came to describe the "normal" people who attended the New York Renaissance Faire in Tuxedo New York (around 1994-95), when people started making fangs. The term found its way through the Clan's glossary of terminology into the New York City Vampire subculture at Long Black Veil.

No longer are the cheerleaders and jocks abusing those who dress differently in mundane high schools. Instead of talking about the newest band these girls are talking about their crush on their new Vampire boyfriend. If presented right there is a state of admiration and mystery about what We are. Of course if you run around your local high school with cheesy fangs and a cape you will catch some criticism, however the glamour of custom fangs a decade ago put fear into the mundane heart, as well as a sense of curiosity. Today it can help get a date, start a conversation and aid in seduction.

Music

Vampires have a diverse taste in music but overall there are many preferences which range from classical, electro, metal, rock and roll, gothic, industrial, R&B, tribal, electronic, classic rock, jazz and blues to name a few. Music is used for atmospheric effects for lounges or rituals and at events such as the Endless Night Vampire Ball to seal the mood. Basically, the most popular is anything a Black Veil Vampire can dance to with high energy.

Movie soundtracks such as Queen of the Damned, Interview with the Vampire, The Crow, Blade, Fight Club and The Matrix series are highly popular amongst those Vampires of Sabretooth lineage.

Prominent bands personally close to the Family include Inkubus Sukkubus, Godhead, Shadow Reborn, Cult of the Psychic Fetus, The Crüxshadows, Voltaire, Lords of Acid and Theatres des Vampires. Their music relates closely to or is inspired by the Clan including Lords of Acid's "Kiss Eternal" from the 2000 album "Farstucker" and Voltaire's song "The Vampire Club," which humorously mocking the Long Black Veil club. Even though he is long passed on, Jim Morrison of The Doors is very popular amongst Vampires.

Many Vampires love neo-pagan music, drum circles and the tribal elements of ancient cultures revised to the modern day. DJs from across the globe score our events with collections of the most popular Vampire music.

Mystery

hroughout history the vampire has been associated with mystery and secrets. The myths of the unknown lord in the castle who has reigned for centuries, the secrets of immortality or the magickal powers of darkness are all mysterious and empowering tools for the Black Veil Vampire.

Personal mysteries are for the modern Vampire extremely essential; as an illusionist hides in plain sight so does the Vampire, only letting forth enough information to entice or appearing suddenly and disappearing just as quickly. Like the vampires of legend, the Current contains a mysterious element. We love to promote Mystery and never reveal too much. We see this - the suspension of belief and curiosity the world has for the Vampire - when we wear our fangs for the first time.

Secrets are a core element of these Mysteries - the Vampire tribe and Family are united by them. With the current vampire craze, vampires can appear on television, write books, and have freedom to live publicly, as the whole world now loves the vampire. Are they just a myth? Or is there a reality that defies old presumptions?

Names (sobriquets)

Names for Vampires are personal and descriptive titles and thus they will often choose a "Nightside / Vampire name" known as a "Sobriquet." This is the pseudonym which they are addressed by within the Vampire community and this name is often chosen by the Vampire or given to them by a person who brought them into the Family or by their Fang-smith.

Like in the Mafia one will often earn their named Sobriquet or have an older member of the Family develop a name based from inspirations of the subject's character or place they were first introduced to the Vampire community. Choosing an appropriate name is a big decision as this will usually stick with the individual their entire life and beyond.

Addressing someone by their chosen Sobriquet is polite, respectful and courteous, especially when interacting amongst Vampires. It is considered rude, disrespectful and an invasion of privacy to another to address someone as their "mundane name" amongst the community.

Sobriquets are used to maintain a separation between day life and night life as well as protect the privacy and aid in the Awakening of an individual by adopting a chosen name. Wisdom dictates choosing a name from ancient languages, deities, heroes or simply made up ones. Names coming from role-playing games and video games are usually considered distasteful and humorous. Remember: names are power, so choose wisely.

Narcissism

The Black Veil Vampire should have a big and healthy ego. Many love to have their pictures taken, dress up, look great, and dress well – these are all expressions of this trait. However, at the same time the Vampire can be kind, pleasurable to be around and very cordial. Their ego is healthy and not one which tramples on others; it is a strong personality and a love of themselves without putting down others.

This Black Veil of Narcissism, the love of the Self, however, is different than the negative mundane perspective on this concept. Looking into the mirror is a favorite hobby of many Black Veiled Vampires. We worship our egos, but not in a senseless and immature way. Instead we seek and nurture healthy and positive relationships with ourselves and others.

The Self is an important element of Vampirism, feeling good about who and what We are, being empowered by the Black Veils and taking care of our own business, life and personal responsibility for our actions. We seek to empower ourselves without oppressing others. We are giving and kind, yet focus on our own survival.

Nightklad

ightklad means to be only clothed in darkness, wearing nothing besides a few pieces of jewelry and a mask. As with many mundane taboos, fledgling Vampires may find this best used in solitary ritual, as couples or amongst groups of individuals who are well acquainted with each other and comfortable with nudity. More advanced Vampires see the benefits of such a practice and are not bound by mortal taboos.

Wearing nothing but darkness is an excellent way to experience and stimulate the free flow of energies and the mind. Being Nightklad helps create a psychological freedom seldom experienced elsewhere. However, the proper use of being Nightklad amongst Vampires in rituals is always make sure that nudity is used for ritual intent and not abused by those who might try to manipulate others or induce unwanted sexual situations. In no ritual should any Vampire be "forced" to be nightklad.

The modern pagan equivalent of nightklad is skyclad which is a literal term from Sanskrit term digambara, which is used in Jainism and Tantra. Gerald Gardner introduced it to Western culture's modern Wiccan practices in the 1950s after spending years with the Jains, whose priests have forsaken clothing.

Nightside

The Nightside is the subjective and subtle reality beyond the five senses and mundane world. This is the "Vampire World", in which a vampire can assume their true personality and awaken to their true nature, free of mundane chains. Most Vampires ritualistically enter the most basic levels of the Nightside by changing their style of dress, choosing a "Nightside" or "Vampire Name,," and keeping a balance so their Dayside life is kept separate. However some Vampires seek more of a connection with the Nightside, and venture beyond the basics into the deeper meanings of magic, spirituality, esotericism, the paranormal, and supernatural.

Elements of this paradigm include: spirits, magic, dreams, occult, ritual, sorcery, subtle reality, aura, reincarnation, chakras, and energy work. In order to master the Nightside perspective, one must have a solid Dayside to objectively gauge results and not get lost into the fantasy of the Vampire Mythos. The Nightside Family is the spiritual or "Vampire Family", where an individual's connection to others is through the spiritual and philosophical instead of physical. Most Vampires only slightly touch the Nightside realm through basic feeding and energy work techniques; truly advanced Vampires move deeper into this paradigm through various forms of initiation and ascension.

Nobility

he Black Veil of personal Nobility states that all those in the Sabretooth Clan must uphold themselves as Lords and Ladies. However, unlike mortal aristocracy, Black Veil Vampires see nobility as a responsibility which must be displayed through action and word.

Many real life aristocrats in Europe have gone through the Rite of Transformation, and even with this they are equal amongst those who have experienced the Rite as they respect the Vampire principles of Privacy. This is akin to being masked while attending Venetian Carnival where everyone is free of their "normal lives" and embraces a new persona, one that gives them freedom. Even they respect Black Veils or risk revealing their personal lives.

Vampire Nobility is of a personal venture, this means carrying oneself with self respect, dressing classy, honoring those who deserve honor, being civil, chivalrous, courteous and living with virtue. This is what the Vampire Nobility Veil promotes. Vampires are elite because they are unique, different from the rest of the world, but they must also set an example and live within the reality we all share.

Nephilim

he legends of the Nephilim are often associated with vampires. According to the Christian Bible, the Nephilim are the offspring of the "sons of god" and the "daughters of men." Some Christian sources say the Nephilim originated from mating between angels and human women. Others say they are the offspring of Seth, the brother of Cain and Abel who rebelled against god, or the children of Cain. In the Bible they also appear as giants who inhabited Canaan. Some passages speak of them as the predators of humanity, whilst others say they were "the heroes of old and men of renown."

The word Nephilim comes from the Sumerian word Nfl, which refers to the Sumerian gods, the Annunaki, whose creators were Ki the earth goddess and An, the sky god. Legends of the origins of the Annunaki parallel those of the Nephilim; they were born of a union between a powerful spirit being and a human woman and their children were blessed with beauty, wisdom, and mystical abilities. According to some of the myths, the Annunaki were teachers and rulers who gave civilization, agriculture, and language to humankind, thus associating them with the Greek story of Prometheus.

The symbol common to the Annunaki is similar to the Egyptian ankh: a horizontal line that represents the horizon and a circle that represents the sunrise or sunset. These symbols can be seen on the Burney Relief. The legends of the Nephilim and Anuanaki may be the origin of the concept of the "holy bloodline" or Sang Grael, which some Vampires traditions attribute to having "Vampire Potential."

Otherkin

There are those who believe they are "Otherkin", or have a soul that is not human. Although most Otherkin are not Vampires or identify within the Vampire Culture, they seem to exist side by side. Being Otherkin is an integral part of some groups or traditions within the Vampire Culture and some even consider the cause of vampirism to be from being Otherkin.

Otherkin can range from those who just believe their soul is something different to fringe concepts like having the soul of a mythical creature like a faerie or a dragon. The Otherkin community is diverse and with many perspectives. Some Otherkin believe they resemble these beings, and embody their archetypes through behavior or even physical appearance

Ouroboros

he Vampiric Dragon Ourboros is one of the three main Black Veil symbols to represent the spiritual and metaphysical nightside. This symbol represents self-reflection and the ability to constantly recreate oneself, an eternal return, similar to the phoenix. To the Black Veil Vampire the Ouroboros depicts a dragon choking on its own tail around its throat, slightly different than more mundane interpretations of the symbol. For Vampires, this represents an ending to the cycle of death and rebirth, continuing in current incarnation as an immortal being.

Frequently the Ouroboros has been represented in many religious systems, including the Egyptian Book of the Dead, and is a common symbol in alchemy and in the search for the Philosopher's Stone. Gnostic and Hermetic spiritual systems also employ the Ouroboros and Swiss psychiatrist Carl Jung interpreted this as of significance for the human psyche.

For the Vampire the Ouroboros's reptilian symbolism and relation to a serpent reflects the Dragon itself. What is most interesting is the symbol of the ancient Ordo Dracul or Order of the Dragon of which the historical Dracula Vlad Tepesh was a member, as it was similar in design to the Ouroboros.

Passion

Vampires hold the Black Veil of Passion as a core virtue of their nature and are often very intense, sensitive, enthusiastic, and emotional beings, yet guided by reason and rational thought without belief. They love to feel and experience all the world has to offer as it shows the Vampire they are alive and have such passion for life that they seek immortality and eternity to fulfill their passions. Passion is a positive, enthusiastic and compelling longing or desire for something or someone. This can be a romantic relationship, art, culture, music, dance, cause, subject, idea or feeling. William Blake said "About how most mundane desire is as a flickering candle flame, yet ours is that of a raging forest a flame?"

As the French author Nicolas Chamfort once said, "Men of reason have endured; men of passion have lived." which very much endorses this Black Veil. The Vampire lives and explores the world with a passion, which is a dark flame, exploring the hidden secrets and unlimited possibilities life has to offer. There is only one life to the Vampire, here, now and in the moment, yet they realize that there is no scientific evidence of an afterlife and through reason will use that to empower their passion for life.

Thus the Sabretooth Vampire through the Black Veils seeks the positive. They are not ruled by their passions as the mundane are, instead they are driven by them and yet guided by reason and rational thoughts before belief. Passion strongly relates to the Veils of Romance, Love and Sensuality.

Primal

hrough this Black Veil a Vampire seeks to develop a strong connection and awareness of their primal nature. Thus acknowledging and recognizing their natural animalistic instincts which are often burried in the mundane mind. Dulled by eons of civilization and often harmed and discouraged by modern society.

This Black Veil takes the inspiration from the noble and honorable predators of the wild such as the wolf, lion, bear, hawk, owl, tiger and shark that puts survival of the self as the highest of all priorities, yet never kills or tortures for pleasure, only survival. Vampires acknowledge that humans are just highly evolved animals. Many Vampires often strongly relate spontaneously to a signature totem or spirit animal, which represents their own personality.

When an individual gets to see their fangs in the mirror at their first fangsmithing session there is often a primal Awakening. The primal element shows when the metamorphosis takes place and some newly awakened Vampires growl and howl at themselves in the mirror unleashing their inner beast!

Primal nature and its acknowledgement is summed up in a relationship with the concept of the Vampire Higher Self known as the Dragon, which represents the philosophical equivalent of the reptilian brain, the most primitive and core element of all vertebrates, including the human.

Privacy

mongst the Vampire's common sense tradition states that confidentiality and privacy should be a guiding principle and an example of the Current is that privacy should be just that! Private. This is one of the main purposes of choosing a pseudonym; a Nightside Name known as a "Sobriquet." It is considered common courtesy and respect to address someone by this chosen name when attending events, interacting online or amongst the Vampire community.

The world loves Vampires, however not all have the luxury of displaying their interests to their birth family, coworkers and friends. Some would simply not understand due to their cultural conditioning. Some of us are "out of the coffin" and exist as promoters. Fangsmiths, nightlife personalities, artists, musicians, performers and so on. Even then we use these stage names that reflect what we are doing.

It is the responsibility of all those who uphold these principles to address someone by their chosen name. It is also the responsibility of individuals to think in advance and reveal their chosen names as they wish to be addressed. If an individual wishes to not reveal their private lives, it is disrespectful and wrong to expect this of them. The only time such names should be revealed or personal information is taken is when legal business is conducted, such as ordering plane tickets, booking hotel rooms, signing contracts or dealing with criminal issues.

Potential

otential refers to the possibility to Awaken to embrace and understand Vampire philosophy and spirituality through Xepher. Full potential exists within only a few humans. It does not appear in the physical DNA but is a spark that lies within the subtle body or spirit of the individual. Potential often skips generations and thus cannot be traced by conventional means. It can be sensed as the "Radiance" or the subtle signature of the Awakening.

Those with potential will often show signs of potental through Xepher without even knowing it, such as unconscious feeding, psychic abilities, unusual empathy, a strong instinct for survival, the desire for Immortality, and a deep love of culture and life.

Rumors of historical orders of Vampires existed to aid those with Potential. They acted as "outreach programs" and undertook various activities to find those with Potential and aid them in their Awakening. Of course the best of these groups never sought to force or coerce Potentials. Only a few of those who actually have Potential will be able to Awaken.

Reality

hat is a Vampire from our perspective and in reality you might ask? The Black Veils are a spiritual and philosophical movement. The foundation of the Black Veils is based upon embracing positive and empowering characteristics of the Vampire Archetype and rejecting the negatives. Black Veil Vampires maintain a firm and grounded Dayside Perspective and live in a rational, objective reality.

Within these pages we specifically talk about the Vampires of the Sabretooth Clan and their characteristics, traits, traditions and virtues. This text is to share not only with Clan members but to reveal and share our own Current with the world.

First and foremost we are to dispel some of the misconceptions of our kind. Vampires do not in the perspective of mundane sense fly, turn into bats, mist or wolves, need to drink blood to survive, have superhuman strength, sleep in coffins, get burned by sunlight or do not age.

They are a unique and diverse set of human beings known as Vampires who have been touched by the Current and Vampire Archetype through getting fangs and thus initiated into the Family of Fang clients.

Red

ed for the Vampire is symbolic of Life, Sacrifice and Blood. The Vampire draws upon the powerful other symbolisms of this color which represent fire, heroism, vitality, vigor, birth, beauty, passion, lust, physical energy, strength, courage, enthusiasm and sex. For the Vampire red is deeply symbolic and use of this color increases and stimulates the mind, spirit and sexuality.

Anytime red is lacking in the spectrum due to human genetic programming, which came from the ability to distinguish ripe fruits from rotten ones, it can be depressing. Caution, however, if red is overused with mortals it can lead to anger, fear, arguments and hatred. Insurance companies often even charge more for bright red cars because they are attention getters and police most often will pull a red sports car over vs. any other color. Red is also used on many flags and in political and spiritual movements and can represent a martyrdom or sacrifice.

Red Mass

The Red Mass is a ceremonial ritualized Vampiric Communion of the Current, Family, and Black Veils, most often for group ritual. The Red Mass is a theatrical ritual (High Magic) that needs a series of psychological tools to aid in ritual and focus energy.

The Red Mass includes elements of ritual similar to hermetic, pagan, ancient mysteries, ceremonial magick and even modern Judo-Christian rituals. Group rituals should be presided over by a Vampire Priest/ess. This rite comes in a multitude of scripts and templates in secret books of the Black Veils.

During the ritual participants arrive as representatives of the Vampire with sigilia, fangs, masks, robes or simply dressed nightklad, only in darkness. Lit by red ambient lighting and candles. This element of theater aids in the flows of energies.

There are three phases of a Red Mass, which include PRELUDE, THE WORKING and AFTER. Most rituals contain those three elements.

The Red Mass, which should only be held in a private chamber such as a cave, private dwelling or grove in the forest away from the eyes of mortals. The only exception is when a Vampire Ball or Vampire Court / Salon is taking place or during the nights of Halloween when the mortal mind is opened to the Current.

Ritual

When most people think of rituals they often think of some dark ceremony, when in fact almost every set of actions performed for symbolic value is a ritual. The very act of getting fangs made is a ritual; celebrating Christmas or a major holiday is also a ritual. These rituals reflect the traditions of a community or culture. Vampires are into rituals; the act of getting fangs is a Rite of Passage for many in the Vampire community to symbolize their involvement.

Often those alien to the traditions who are observing a ritual will not understand what is going on as they are not educated about the ceremony. However examples such as voodoo rituals are popular in New Orleans or Indian rituals on reservations. The projection of the ritual seems to be mystical and enlightening to the observer. Whilst the insiders are "emic" as they know the purpose and course of the rite, they are thus being involved from an educated view. Handshakes, rites of passage, oaths of allegiance, coronations of Kings or Queens, Christmas shopping, Halloween parties, dance recitals, sporting events, high school proms, graduations, marriages, funerals, veterans parades and even the 4th of July are all rituals for a community.

Within the Vampire subculture there are many rituals beyond going through the Rite of Passage obtaining a pair of fangs. Another example is the Red Mass, which ceremonially projects the symbolism of the Black Veils in a theatrical and psychodramatic format. There are also other rituals such as celebrating Vampire Holidays, Vampire Weddings (Blood & Roses) or most notably going to the Vampire Ball. Thus the Vampire culture like any other culture is defined by its rituals.

Rock & roll

ampires ROCK!" is a statement of the relationship Vampires have with the history, culture and attitude surrounding this style of music. Rock and roll started in its embryonic stages as a culture and music which began in the 1920s and 30s in the United States but eventually evolved as a worldwide influence ever since.

Vampires relate to this concept by living in a way that is very much like an individual rock star without the overflowing ridiculous ego. When we rock out, it means to live life to its fullest and having fun, being happy and celebrating life whilst challenging the status quo.

Vampire Music reflects this stage with Vampires often loving the sources of the music that now today inspire or create the entire rock scene. You will find today's Vampires in glam rock parties, concerts and even gothic clubs dancing and celebrating with a vitality which rivals others, then often going home to their mundane lives and children. Sabretooth often state clearly that "We are not selling out, We are rockin' out!"

Romance

O ne of the most expressive of the Black Veils is Romance. This mysterious and pleasurable expression of a connection between beloved individuals requires action, passion and love. The Vampire seeks to experience these connections in an ever-expanding exploration of new and creative ways of expression. Vampire romance is not just restricted to lovers; it can also be an appreciation of adventure and experience or a deep-rooted passion for a particular subject, art or culture.

For the Vampire, Romance is a spiritual act and experience, one empowered by the Veils of Seduction, Life and Love. Vampires also build the tension of romance through the Mystery and Seduction Veils, resulting in a courtship that is not often directly expressed.

Romanticism is always part of the allure of the Vampire. We love to love. We love to seduce, we love to dance and charm those around Us. Having deep relationships with our lovers and friends is as essential as looking at a painting or enjoying a walk down the streets of a beloved city. Many a young girl has envisioned her favorite Hollywood vampires like Lestat, Eric the Viking, or Dracula, seducing her with forbidden courtships. Such fantasies have only empowered our reality.

Ronin

onin are solitary and or independent Vampires who are not affiliated to or participating with any Vampire family, organization, house, or court. The term ronin comes from the history of feudal Japan, and refers to a wandering samurai who has no lord or master. The term was added to the Black Veils lexicon and Vampire Culture in 1997, during the era of the Long Black Veil for the vampires attending the club who weren't affiliated. Ronin may study and agree with the Black Veils, and identify with them on their own terms, or have their own perspectives. Ronin are often free spirits who are intimately familiar with the Current, culture, spirituality, traditions, and philosophy of Vampire Culture, and of the different perspectives on Vampirism.

While there are many different types of ronin, there are four types that are common in Vampire Culture: "Original Ronin" are those who have not completed any formal rites of passage or initiated into the into any family.. "Gone Ronin" are those who have chosen to abandon their affiliations to a group. "Forced Ronin" are those who have been banished from a family or court. "Ronin Spirits" may still be affiliated with or initiated to a court or house, but are still independent, and their level of involvement rises and falls; much like cats, ronin spirits follow their own whims.

Sabretooths

he Sabretooth Clan is the world's largest and one of the world's largest and best known Family of individuals drawn to the Vampire lifestyle, with its own culture, traditions and history. Founded on August 7th, 1995 this collection of like-minded individuals quickly evolved its own distinct culture which has greatly influenced and inspired the worldwide Vampire Culture. All had a free forum to evolve into a common Current.

Sabretooths, members of the Sabretooth Clan, are individuals who share the common experience of having had fangs made for them by the Founder. Having fangs made is known as "The Rites of Transformation." This rite of passage is about more than just being fitted with a custom pair of fangs; incorporated are mysterious elements including the "Oath," "the Mirror," the "Oracle," the "Naming," and the "Ankh." Sabretooths hail from many diverse backgrounds, including practicing the Vampire lifestyle in many formats, vampire scholars and Black Swans who are educated on Vampire Culture but yet not yet fully identify as one. Those who truly embrace this transformative milestone are united in a uniquely tribal and Family spirit.

The first Sabretooth was Lady N, who had her fangs made on Christmas Day 1994. She is actually Father Sebastiaan's birth mother, and became the first and only "Brood" of that year. Brood is a term referring to the year a Sabretooth went through the Rites of Transformation. Since that first year, each subsequent year's Brood have gone through the ever-evolving Transformation Rite, while getting their fangs made in places such as the FangShop in NYC, European music festivals, the Paris Catacombs, in the House of Blues courtyard in New Orleans, and many other cities around the world.

Sacrifice

he word sacrifice comes from the Latin sacrificium or "sacred rites" and the old French "to do, perform" and refers in mortal-minded terms to offerings of animals, plants, money, gifts or even living humans to the divine in exchange for favors.

Vampires respect free will of sentient beings and never harm animals or humans physically. What is inefficient for the Vampire to do is to destroy life. We are catalysts of the flow of life and murder of an animal or human is the destruction of life as a source.

Animals and children do not have the proper level of awareness to make a choice regarding personal sacrifice. So they shall not be harmed or hurt; only those who offer up their own life energies with a proper free will shall be able to offer their life.

Sanguine

The term "sanguine" in Latin means blood. Although the Sabretooth Clan does not officially endorse or promote drinking of human blood at our events or amongst our membership. This term refers to "sanguine vampires" or "sanguinarians" who partake in the act of drinking physical human blood.

For most this is a ritualistic and sexual act (fetish). It is true the vast majority of Vampires do not fall into this category or this practice. Ideally, Sanguines perform this rite within the context of safe, sane, consensual, and monogamous relationships where both partners are tested and remain "fluid bound." Sadly some Sanguines go on television and media to sensationalize a highly sacred act, which should remain out of the public eye and behind closed doors.

Blood drinking often has psychological side effects of creating deep spiritual links and may for a while create a co-dependence for a while. There is also at this time no scientific or psychological evidence that humans benefit nutritionally or health wise from consuming each other's blood. In fact, current evidence points to the opposite perspective; that drinking blood can be extremely dangerous if not done properly. However there are actual scientific studies going on at this time to discover the purpose and reality of these urges. Just be cautious and responsible consenting adults.

Scholars

The scholars are mostly non-Vampires who have become world experts on the Vampire mythology and the culture surrounding it. Notable examples include Dr. J. Gordon Melton (The Vampire Book), Katherine Ramsland (author of Piercing the Darkness and Anne Rice biographer), Rosemary Ellen Guiley (Vampires Among Us), Elizabeth Miller (Transylvanian Society of Dracula / Vampire Empire), Dax Stoker (The Vampire Historian) and many more.

Each has written scholarly essays for academic journals, many have PHDs or a deep interest in the the subject and phenomena of the Vampire Culture. Most are very respectful but some are biased, and all make great effort to properly explain their perspectives.

Secrets

Secrets protect and bind Us, our Mysteries are our own, and those who wish to explore them should seek them out alone, through personal initiative and action. As a sleight of hand magician employs the principle of "hidden in plain sight," so does the Black Veil Vampire.

First, follow the example set by elder members of the Sabretooth Family. Honor other Vampires' right of privacy, such as in respect to their mundane identity. Never disclose their personal information to anyone, especially to the mortal-minded, but even to other Family members, without their explicit permission. The only circumstance under which We should disclose the given name and identity of any Vampire is if such information was required under the legal jurisdiction of the proper authorities.

Second, try to keep an air of mystery, avoiding open discussion of the Black Veils in public, the media or with those not of the Family. At all times speak only for yourself and never represent the greater Family other than directing someone in the right direction to find a Fangsmith. Leave that to those select members of the Family who are properly trained and experienced in public relations. Supporting this Black Veil furthers the Glamour and protects the Mysteries.

Finally, one of the most important aspects of this principle of the Vampire Secrets Veil is avoiding discussion of the Mysteries with someone who has not had the opportunity to read this book or get fangs and had time to reflect on the experience. Respect free will and let Seekers gain a first impression of the Mysteries and formulate an opinion on their own. When an individual has the opportunity to experience it for themselves, they shall draw their own conclusions, whilst if you tell them about it, they will more likely only be able to see it from your perspective.

Seduction

In the modern "Vampire Mythos", the Vampire is beautiful, charming, and most of all seductive. Of all the Black Veils, Seduction is a tool that the Vampire uses to entice others into freely coming to an agreement. Seduction is often sexual in nature although that is not always the case. Enticement is the center of seduction. The Western world knows famous seducers such as Casanova, Marilyn Monroe or the God Eros who are prime role models which the Vampire can draw upon, as well as using historical personalities and others from mythology.

Seduction can be used beyond the realm of the Vampire World - it can be used to further one's life i.e. when the Vampire wishes to obtain a mate, entice another to come into agreement with their views, or to promote a concept. For example in the 1950s former president Charles de Gaulle of France came out of retirement to help prevent a civil war in Algeria. To do this he seduced the French people by donning his WWII uniform and employing the new medium of television. Through Seduction he freed Algeria of the French generals and avoided a major conflict.

On the other hand in its primary state, Seduction is an enticement through sexual arousal, leading to a decision that would not be made otherwise. The Vampire relies on this Black Veil and it is best projected through what is known as the Glamour, using aids such as Neuro Linguistic Programming (NLP), images, sensory stimulation and stimulating discoveries of a subject's desires. Mythological examples include the Lilitu demons of Sumerian legends as they come in sexual dreams and the Incubi and Succubi who feed upon the lifeforce of humans through sexual stimulation.

Selfishness

You cannot love others unless you love yourself first. The Vampire is Selfish, this is a Vampire virtue, and the Self is the most important individual; virtually one is one's own personal god. Individual success, interests and love come first for the Self; personal survival is above all else.

Selfishness is completely acceptable; however it should be done not with an ego of putting down others, but with one of self-improvement, evolution and a dedication to personal interests. There is no shame for the Vampire in being selfish as it is completely normal.

Financial security, spiritual evolution, and all other pursuits should benefit the individual and are inherently selfish. Doing something nice for someone else makes you feel good. Getting a university education improves your self as well as your earning potential. Having a job you like is essential; happiness and contentment are personal priorities. We have children to have the satisfaction of being a parent. To deny this reality is simply foolish! Humans are naturally selfish, working for their own personal interests which always come first.

Sensuality

he Vampire Sensuality Black Veil states that the Vampire loves the corporeal world and all the pleasures within which can be experienced by the five senses. Vampires are drawn to the beautiful patterns, smells, sounds, tastes and sights.

With these "Vampire Eyes" the Vampire sees first the beauty in humanity, nature, darkness and the Universe. Most of all, Vampires enjoy the pleasures of amazing foods, feeling the wind on their skin, the magnificence of a sunset, or the diversity of smells that exist in creation.

Being sensual, Vampires love the experiences of life from the Dragon's Eyes. They love to look at a beautiful piece of architecture, studying amazing works of art, taking a sensual bath, making love, touching amazing fabrics, feeling the earth below their feet, listening to unique sounds of music and the chorus of nature, never ignoring that it may all end and to take in as much as possible in life.

Silver

Unlike vampires in fiction in reality silver is not just about the material, but what it represents. Most Vampires who become members of the Sabretooth Clan and Vampire culture commonly state, "I prefer and love silver." Yet gold is popular for its divine and immortalist symbolism.

Silver is an essential color for the Vampire as it is more welcoming to the lunar concept of the moon. It is symbolic of purity for the Vampire. Most Vampires prefer silver over gold for personal purposes and for meditation.

Symbolically relating to the Moon, silver also represents a reflection of light, similar to gold but almost the color of the moon. With this reflectivity it is very interesting to see how silver is feminine, reflective and similar to a mirror and thus reflecting the soul of the Current.

Spirit

he Vampire Spirit refers to the massive collective energies, experiences and agreement of the "Vampire Mythos" in the public minds eye. The more private and internal version of the Vampire Spirit the expanded "Current" which is the internal experience of collective consciousness that manifests in the entire Vampire Culture.

Very much like a unifying team spirit or the collective cultural identity of a country or family. the Vampire Spirit is strong and fueled by the ancient legends. modern literature. film and television and the fact almost every culture has a Vampire mythos.

Individuals who go through the Rites of Transformation in its current form or the past have been touched by this Spirit in part or whole and are able to experience the Current. The simple Rite of Passage of getting fangs is enough to have an experience few in the world could ever have imagined. This uniting factor is one of the most fundamental and empowering aspects of this Spirit.

There are deeper, more esoteric interpretations used by some of the internal activities of the Clan. however they are not something to be discussed within the scope of this text.

Sports

any laugh when they hear of the idea of Vampire Sports - this Black Veil is as serious as any other. What is a Vampire Sport? Any sport the Vampire performs in healthy competition, to challenge the individual as well as increase health and vitality of the Self. Some Vampires can be good team players, but most are more like cats than dogs: not into team efforts.

So Vampire Sports include things like snowboarding, skiing, surfing, belly dancing, SCUBA, equestrian, archery, shooting at the gun range, dance, fire spinning, cliff diving, tennis, squash and so on.

When competing, they are competing against themselves instead of others. The goal of Vampire Sports is to improve the Self and compete only against the limits imposed upon the individual.

Stones

Stones within the Vampire Legacy Ankh represent one's time within the Legacy. Many will confuse them with a hierarchy and status, but stone colors are a measure of time since their Rites of Transformation (the fang ceremony.) There are absolutely no formal status or privilages that come with these titles. to improve the Self and compete only against the limits imposed upon the individual. These titles are only valid and recognized within the Sabretooth Clan and not with any other vampire organization or group.

WHITE STONE - New fledglings to the Family, from their Rites of Transformation until a year and a day after. They are usually new and inexperienced Sabretooths usually becoming familiar with the Black Veils.

RED STONE - There has been a year and a day from their Rites of Transformation. They have celebrated a FangDay on the anniversary of their fanging and are encouraged to be well versed on the Veils.

PURPLE STONE - Five years and a day have passed since their Rites of Transformation. They are seasoned and often knowledgeable in the Black.

BLACK STONE - Long-term members of the Legacy who have celebrated 13 years since their Transformation. Ancients are usually very well versed experts in the Black Veils.

Survival

his Black Veil encompasses personal survival, the ability to preserve the Self and move through life with not just primal needs but ultimate success and experience. The Vampire seeks to reduce life's health risks with preventative medicine, self-defense techniques, and other methods of self-care and self-improvement.

At the same time the Vampire is not some paranoid individual just avoiding risks. The Vampire is merely managing them objectively and realistically. Quitting smoking also reduces many health risks. Making wise financial investments and obtaining health insurance are essential to a long, healthy, and prosperous life.

If it is legal to obtain a weapon for self-defense or take a martial arts course, this is wise. Learning how to survive in the wilderness and security procedures are also essential elements when one can least expect it. You never know. Be prepared, be ready and realize that survival of the Self is the highest principle of Black Veil Vampirism.

tattoos (ezerix)

attooing has long been a rite of passage in many cultures. Members of the modern primitives scene embrace tattoos as important markers of personal empowerment. While not all Vampires choose to adorn themselves with Ezerix, or magical tattoos, designing and obtaining such symbols can be a powerful magickal tool.

Examples of Ezerix most often include the Legacy Ankh, Pulse Veves, personal sigils, or marks from rites of passage such as devotion, initiations or passions. Ezerix may include subtle and small tattoos behind the ears, under the hairline, or on the back of the neck as well as large images on back, legs, or arms. Ezerix serve as signs of commitment to the Black Veils and may be used as focal points during ritual and magickal workings.

What makes an Ezerix powerful is that charging of these glyphs or sigilia goes beyond the physical body. The image is actually engraved into the subtle body or is already on the subtle body as would be a birthmark bestowed by a patron during conception. The ritual for creating Ezerix is a secret of the Sabretooth Flame. The creation and acceptance of an Ezerix denotes a profound magical commitment. However, it is not uncommon for a previously existing tattoo to be later charged as an Ezerix.

titles

ithin the VC we sometimes see aristocratic titles like Lord / Lady, King / Queen, Sir / Madame, Elder and so on. Far more common in America (and less so in Europe), titles are mostly used among lifestyle Vampires. Titles within the VC are either "Theatrical titles" which are for roleplaying, fun, and enhancing glamour, or actual "Job titles" (Gatekeeper, Host, VIP director, Treasurer, Stage Manger), which have actual positions, duties, and responsibilities. Sometimes Job Titles will have a theatrical counterpart such as Event Director is "Vizier."

Theatrical titles can be fun but it's very important to remember the adage "the title doesn't make the man, the man makes the title." Titles are way too often taken far too seriously, and can become abusive or go to the bearer's head. Titles are bestowed by one's peers and are best not self-proclaimed. Michael Jackson never called himself "King of Pop." In the early years, the Sabretooth Clan experimented with titles but no longer formally recognize theatrical titles within or outside the Clan. We use stone colors to mark how long a member has been in the Family and we assign specific job titles as needed.

The mature and advanced Vampire has little need for a title, and only uses one when working a job or having fun being theatrical and roleplaying at an event. The advanced Vampire is a majestic, confident, charismatic, educated, cultured, magical, and empowered individual. Rule yourself, with mastery of the Black Veils. Knowledge and application defines a Vampire, not a title. Live with Nobility, Chivalry, Honour, Love, Passion, Magic, and Culture ; put down the hubris. Every Vampire who does so will be a true King or Queen / Lord or Lady through actions not words or titles.

transhuman

Vampires are often drawn to the Black Veil of Transhumanism and the transhumanist movement, which is the concept of evolving the human condition through emerging technologies to eliminate and/or overcome current limitations. Specific concepts include drastically slowing or eliminating aging, enhancing mental and physical abilities and improved interactions with technology.

Such technologies of note include exploring cryonics, longevity, biotechnology, implants, experimental medicines, merging with technologies such as cybernetics and the like. What makes the Vampires embrace this Veil is that such powers mimic the vampires of mythology, legend and fiction in a potential real world application and is inspiration for transhumanism.

Many members of the mundane world may consider such actions unnatural or against religious beliefs, however there is a natural curiosity and openness within the Vampyre community to embracing and almost welcoming of the concepts of transhumanism. Look to the writings of FM-2030 of the New School in New York City or futurist Max More or immortalist Aubrey de Grey.

tribal

Vampires who follow the Black Veils are highly Family oriented and have a strong sense of kinship. Thus they are tribal as they are united by a common Current of agreement through common experiences, perspectives and the Rites of Transformation.

The members of the Sabretooth Clan come from many walks of life, almost every social group, economic, ethnic, spiritual and philosophical perspective. What unites them is their common spirit, which makes them a tribe.

Sometimes the Clan has been humorously called the "Vampire Mafia" by those with a good sense of humor, of the resulting network of individuals whose kinship brings them onto a unique perspective on life. What makes this special is that We have artists, performers, doctors, executives, politicians, lawyers, taxi drivers, college professors, engineers, hotel concierges, dancers, bus drivers etc. all sharing such a profound adventure in life that they often pool their talents, connections and resources in an effort to support other members and in support of the Clan.

Being Tribal does not mean Vampires are followers. This is far from the case. They are highly independent and individualistic yet at the same time often highly social in spurts, and they love nothing more than socializing with others of the Vampire Spirit.

twilight

The Black Veil of Twilight is not about sparkling vampires lost in some romantic story; it is about much, much more. Twilight is about contrast and balance, the equilibrium between the Dayside and the Nightside, where only results matter.

The Dayside is the "Mundane World" of the rational, materialistic experience, whilst the Nightside refers to the "Vampire World" of the mystical and spiritual elements of Vampire philosophy and metaphysics. Both are contained individually and when separated then both applied, the result is living or "coming forth by Twilight." Here both sides are relevant and equally as important.

In its most simplistic form an example of Twilight is a Vampire who is ill and wishes to get better efficiently and quickly. First they will work from the Dayside, going to the doctor to and make sure that all normal scientific procedures are attended to, whilst they will simultaneously go and mediate and seek holistic and spiritual healing. Together both sides will result in a Twilight, which leads to covering all the bases. The goal of the Vampire is to live in a balanced Twilight, not just limited to the Dayside or Nightside, but both.

Valentine's

alentine's Day, or more appropriately "Anti-Valentine's Day" or "Crimson Festival" amongst the Vampires, is celebrated on or around (the most convenient day to celebrate and party) February 14. From the Vampire's perspective this night is the time when We celebrate our deepest passions and romances, as well as past and present loves.

Here we recognize the partnerships and marriages that helped us in our personal evolutions. The Crimson Festival is also a festival of the Hunt, celebrating its seductive, civilized, and glamorous aspects. The symbolism of crimson is related to the concept embodied in the words "For the Blood is the Life," which is a metaphor for sustaining ourselves by feasting on life-force energy. This festival celebrates personal evolutions, as well as the loves and partnerships we are currently engaged in. Here we celebrate, romance, and love.

the Vampire Mythos

The Vampire Mythos is defined in the Black Veils as the collective impact of all of the legends, film, literature, fantasy and mythology related to the vampire from all time periods. From ancient times almost every culture has included some sort of vampiric mythological figure in their superstitions and lore, ranging from the Lilitu demons of ancient Sumerian and Jewish myths, the Incubi / Succubi of Medieval folklore, the faerie like Baobhan Sith of the Scottish Highlands, the Strigoi of Romania, the bloodthirsty Gods of Central and South America and the ghoulish predators of Asia and Africa.

These past myths and legends have collectively given rise to our own modern vampire mythos. One can say that this modern mythos began with the Romantic Movement literary work of author John William Polidori; the short story "The Vampyre" published on April 1st 1819, featuring the suave British nobleman vampire character Lord Ruthvan. This more modern view of the vampire was expanded upon in Victorian literature works such as the lurid serialized penny dreadful "Varney the Vampire" (1845-7) and the gothic horror of "Carmilla" (1871). Then all radically changed with the publication of Bram Stroker's "Dracula" in 1897, and from there the Vampire Mythos exploded into mainstream culture in a very refined manner.

The Vampire Mythos was truly defined and evolved in 20th century though thousands of incarnations in film, television, literature, role-playing games (RPGs), video games, merchandise and even spawned an entire vampire lifestyle subculture. The biggest influences of the past 100 years on the Vampire Mythos, aside from Dracula (in films from 1931, 1958, 1979 and 1992), include Barnabas Collins from the gothic daytime drama "Dark Shadows" (1966-71), Anne Rice's Vampire Chronicles novels (Interview with the Vampire published in 1975) and the tabletop role-playing game "Vampire: The Masquerade" (released in 1991). All of these interpretations have influenced and illustrated what a modern vampire can be; that immortal, aristocratic, angelic anti-hero, who is immortal, powerful and highly social yet extremely independent. The Vampire is a powerful being that many of us wish to become, can see reflected in our own primal desires and a monster that we can relate to and many times sympathize with.

This is the modern 21st century Vampire Mythos.

Vampire Philosophy

The Black Veil Vampire acknowledges and trusts their animal instincts and primal nature as to guide them. The Black Veil Vampire seeks to awaken their most inner elements of their Dragon (buried deep under layers of human conditioning) and allow this primal nature to flourish. The Dragon is a symbol of the magickal, evolved, noble predator who is very much in touch with their animalistic nature. For the Vampire it is the symbol of our higher selves. The core of Vampire Philosophy is embracing one's primal nature, destroying the victim mentality, and accepting the laws of nature as a guide for survival. This is the core of Xepher. The evolved Vampire does not believe in torturing or abusing humans or animals. To be truly adept in Vampirism, it is required to fully accept this fundamental principle.

Vampiric Philosophy is similar to Social Darwinism. From the perspective of the Vampire, it is clear that nothing and no one is created equal. As Charles Darwin noted, variation (difference) abounds in nature as well as the human world. Living things that possess variations most favorable or helpful to their survival will survive and pass those advantages to their offspring. Within human society the concept of "favorable variation" is more complex than within the animal and plant kingdom. Humans have the ability to adapt to their circumstances, and change weaknesses into advantages or develop strengths into powerful tools of mastery.

The most successful people are those who use both their inborn talents and develop important skills, such as exceptional musicians, philosophers, artists, and professionals. Consider athletes such as Michael Jordan who are born with a superior body type but must train to master the game. Stephen Hawking had a genius-level intellect, yet suffers from AALS (amyotrophic lateral Sclerosis). He had survived beyond all predictions for his life expectancy and was one of the most brilliant physicists in history. Best-selling writer Stephen King endured years of discouragement and rejection slips until he published his first novel. The Noble Predators of the human culture succeed through inherent advantages, creativity, cunning, determination, and constant hard work, just as the predator must do in the wild.

Walpurgis

alpurgis, or the "Dragon Night", takes place during the night of April 30 or May 1 and falls upon the neo-pagan holiday of Beltane. This celebration began as a pre-Christian European Spring holiday and was later co-opted by the Christians. Traditionally Walpurgisnacht, is the night when demons, faeries, banshees, and other such legendary creatures are said to hold their dark celebrations.

To the Vampires this night represents the fire of the Dragon. This festival is also a major celebration of the Family when the Red Mass is often held between members of the Family and in Vampire Balls around the world.

Warrior

Those who embrace the Black Veil of the Vampire Warrior are consummate protectors and guardians. They are usually drawn to the subjects of strategy, military history, weapons, martial arts and security.

The ethics of this Black Veil is to first avoid violence, using it as a last resort only when all other options fail. Being prepared and educated enough to protect and make everyone safe is the highest purpose of being a Vampire Warrior. The resonance of this Veil is not for everyone, but it is very apparent when someone naturally has this element of the Vampire Current within them through their interests and expressions. For them, this comes naturally.

All Vampires should at least know this Black Veil as a virtue and understand its core concepts. Vampire Warriors often dress with military or martial arts flair, sporting combat boots and vestiges of military uniforms. Collectors of guns and medieval weapons feel a constant need to make sure everyone is safe around them.

Often they will be active in the military, security or police force or at least have some training in either category. The oft-cited "bible" of the Vampire Warrior is Sun Tzu's ancient book "The Art of War."

Werewolves

any think of werewolves as opposed to Vampires in some eternal war as detailed in Vampire the Masquerade games and the Underworld films. In reality, this is just a role-playing and Hollywood concept and not the case with the Vampires of the Sabretooth Clan.

Werewolves of the Clan are not pack animals as one might think; they are highly independent, loyal and primal individuals who are touched by both the Vampire Current and that of the Wolf Spirit simultaneously. When you meet someone who identifies themselves as a werewolf associated with the Clan, they are often very spiritual, gruff and shamanistic, with many similar traits to that of the popular character of Wolverine in X-Men.

The Black Veils personified by the wolves of the Family and are often Primal, Loyal, Romance, Love and even more commonly the Warrior and Vampire Gentleman. They cannot shape shift, grow hair or turn into a wolf man with the full moon in the physical sense, but many will practice techniques of howling and often wear claws and furs to play with lovely ladies or gentlemen.

Will

ill is the lifeblood of the individual Current and an essential Black Veil to fuel Xepher. Without Will there is no success, without Will there is no effort and without Will there is no freedom. Vampires see every challenge as an opportunity and every failure as a lesson and a new opportunity to do better next time. "Hindsight is foresight," they say and each challenge in life is just designed to further the Will.

The Will is something that must be developed, honed and evolved. Athletes use Will to push themselves to the next level, students use Will to get through the most challenging of exams and courses, mothers use Will to give birth, politicians use Will to get elected and artists use Will to create. For the Black Veil Vampire, Will and its development is a powerful tool to embrace and enjoy life with.

Witch

"Vampire Witch" is a powerful archetype of the feminine embracing of the Vampire Current and the Black Veils. This form of Witchery is not inspired by the witch of Halloween with broomsticks, black cats, and cauldrons, but is a philosophy of feminine empowerment.

The Vampire Witch sits upon the throne of the Dragon Goddess Within as a serpent of Draconian inspiration. She scoffs at the cultural limitations placed on women, and uses seduction, charm, cleverness, beauty, sensuality, intellect, alternative thinking, reason, knowledge, and glamour as elements in her life.

The Vampire Witch is Elegant, Seductive, Primal, Romantic, and a genuine Libertine. She never responds to criticism of her business interests, sexual practices, or other choices. She is not afraid to be a lady and enjoy the Flesh and Spirit in whichever portions she chooses. If she wants a person, she goes for them, with aggression, subtly, or some method of her own. Think of a female swashbuckler, Texan cowgirl or a heavy metal rock girl who is elegant and cultured enough so a gent can take her home to meet his conservative parents or to an elegant night at the opera!

Today, more than any other era in history, there is a free place for the Vampire Witch to rule her own dreams, grasp the chalice of life's and rise within a culture which praises the very elements of what she is. Let people worship and respect her, yet return worship and honor to those who naturally or intentionally relate to the Black Veil of the Vampire Gentleman. Many Vampire Witches often wear red or black flowers in their hair and sophisticated yet sexy clothes, to show their feminine tastes, but individual style is always apparent.

Vampire Witches often find these books inspirational: The Satanic Witch by Anton LaVey, French Women Don't Sleep Alone by Jamie Cat Callen, and The Art of Seduction by Robert Greene.

Xepher

epher is the central power word of the Black Veils, and refers to the metamorphosis of Vampiric Awakening, evolution, and transformation of the Self. The term, spelled "Xeper", was brought into modern esoteric usage by the Temple of Set (ToS), and inspired the concept in the Black Veils.

The word comes from the Egyptian "Kheper," which can be translated as "to come into being," "to become", and "transformation". Another source of the word is Khepera, the name for the morning incarnation of the Sun god in Egyptian mythology. Although the term of Xepher has a slightly different phonetic value than the original Egyptian word (the Egyptian word is pronounced khef-fer, and our term is pronounced zhef-hur), it carries a similar definition and meaning. The Xepher of each individual joined in chorus is what empowers the Current.

The associated Egyptian symbol or hieroglyph is a scarab beetle. The scarab beetle lays its eggs in carrion, which gave the Ancient Egyptians the impression that these insects were born from death. Thus, the scarab came to represent rebirth.

Xepher is about self-empowerment, positive energies, creation, material mastery, personal glamour, spiritual Awakening, and living a prosperous, healthy, and long and vital life. For the Black Veil Vampire, Xepher is not just a goal, but also a never-ending constant journey.

Vampire World History
& Sabretooth Chronology

Here is the official timeline and chronology for the "Vampire World History" according to the Black Veils and from the perspective of the Sabretooth Clan. S.Y. designates "Sabretooth Year" which began on August 7th 1995 with the founding of the Sabretooth Clan.   This timeline and chronology will be fleshed out in the book on Vampire World History coming soon in the Black Veils series.

VAMPIRIC PREHISTORY

730CE

The Baital Pachisi, the collection of 25 fables surrounding Vikram the Vampire, is written in Sanskrit by the scholar Bhavbhuti.

1047

The first recorded appearance of the word "upir" in writing referring to the Russian prince as "Upir Lichy," or the "wicked vampire."

1196

The "Chronicles" written by William of Newburgh, records several vampire like revenants in England.

1428

Vlad Dracula "Vlad the Impaler" is born.

1477

Vlad Dracula "Vlad the Impaler" is assassinated.

1484

The Malleus Maleficarium by Heinrich Kramer and Jacob Sprenger is published. It becomes known as the Witch Hunter's Bible and discusses how to hunt and destroy vampires.

1560

Erzsebet (Elizabeth) Bathory is born.

1610

Erzsebet (Elizabeth) Bathory is tried for murdering several hundred young women and sentenced to life-imprisonment.

1614

Erzsebet (Elizabeth) Bathory dies.

1645

Graecorum Opinationibus is written by Greek cleric Leo Allatius, detailing the of the vrykolakas; the vampires of Greece.

1819

The Vampyre, a short novelette is written and published by John William Polidori. The Vampyre is inspired by Lord Byron.

1872

Carmilla by Joseph Sheriden Le Fanu is published.

1897

Dracula written by Bram Stoker is published in London.

1922

*Nosferatu: A Symphony of Horror, directed by F. W. Murnau is released in Germany. This is an unauthorized adaption of Bram Stoker's Dracula. This is the first death of a vampire by direct sunlight.

1930

Psychic Self-Defense written by Dion Fortune is published in London. It contains defense techniques against psychic and astral vampires.

1966

Dark Shadows the TV show featuring the vampire Barnabas Collins first airs. The first time in history a vampire is not a villain. The show airs until 1971.

1969

The Satanic Bible by Anton Szandor LaVey is published with an article "Not

All Vampires Drink Blood," warning about emotional psychic vampirism. The book becomes an instant best seller, outselling the Christian Bible in some cases.

1970

Sean Manchester establishes The Vampire Research Society in the UK. In Search of Dracula by Raymond T. McNally and Radu Florescu is published.

Stephan Kaplan establishes The Vampire Research Center in the UK. "The Highgate Vampire" incident occurs in London, spawning a massive hunt. Reports of a real vampire in the Highgate cemetery are reported.

1975

The Temple of Set (ToS) is formed in July of this year from former members of the Church of Satan. It is what will eventually form the Order of the Vampyre (OOV.)

1976

Anne Rice's Interview with the Vampire is published, igniting a massive interest in people wanting to be vampires.

1976

Martin V Riccardo founds the Vampire Studies group which publishes The Vampire Journal.

1984

The Temple of Set (TOS) officially establishes the Order of the Vampyre (OOV) as a subgroup, being one of the first organizations to bring vampires out of fiction. The OOV's goal is to harness the archetype of the vampire for personal empowerment and occult practices.

1985

Anne Rice's book The Vampire Lestat is published and goes to the best seller list.

The original Fright Night is released, later influencing vampire culture.

1987

The film <u>Near Dark</u>, directed by Kathryn Bigelow is released. One of the early influences on vampire culture.

The film <u>The Lost Boys</u> is released, directed by Joel Schumacher. Very influential on rock and roll vampire imagery.

1989

The Temple of the Vampire (TOV) officially establishes itself as the first legally registered vampire church in the USA and the <u>Vampire Bible</u> is released.

Norine Dresser's book <u>American Vampires : Fans, Victims and Practitioners</u> is published, detailing real life vampires.

1991

Sebastiaan's mother, "Lady N" tells him Tom Cruise is going to play a vampire named "Lestat" and introduces him to Anne Rice's book, <u>Interview with the Vampire</u>.

<u>Vampire: The Masquerade</u> first edition is published by White Wolf Publishing. It wins the 1992 Origins award for best RPG and goes onto a wild success in multiple categories of entertainment including but not limited to TCGs, novels, video games, LARPs and TV. This game is inspired by <u>The Vampire Chronicles</u> by Anne Rice.

1992

Prelude to The Sabretooth Clan:

Whilst attending a medieval live roleplaying game named Xanadra, one of the other players tells Sebastiaan of a Vampire: the Masquerade LARP happening in Harrisburg PA hosted by Night Owl Games.

Elsewhere in the Vampire World:

Francis Ford Coppola's movie "Bram Stoker's Dracula" opens.
Anne Rice's <u>Tale of a Body Thief</u> is published.

1993

Within the The Sabretooth Clan:

Father Sebastiaan after getting involved in the Vampire: The Masquerade community (LARP). November 8th in NJ he gets his first pair of fangs with his lady Dawn in preparation for his high school prom.

Father is presented a Xeroxed copy of the Vampire Bible at the NY Renfaire by "Dimitri" an active member of the group because he turns 18.

Elsewhere in the Vampire World:

Vampire: the Masquerade roleplay is widely popular.

1994

Prelude to The Sabretooth Clan:

Whilst working at Wild Pair shoes in Bridgewater Commons Mall in NJ, Father meets a club promoter from Limelight who sees his fangs and invites him to help run guest lists. Limelight is the hottest club in NYC at the time.

Sebastiaan meets a prosethedonist (dental surgeon) who offers to teach him the art of fangsmithing, and he apprentices for 18 months. These two elements combined together create what will become the Sabretooth (fangs) and Endless Night (events) branches of his business.

On Christmas Day 1994 he makes Lady N. (his birth mother) his first pair of fangs.

Elsewhere in the Vampire World:

November - Interview with the Vampire: The Vampire Chronicles opens with Tom Cruise as Lestat and Brad Pitt as Louis.

Steven Lessing establishes the Vampire Access Line (VAL) for the vampire community in NYC.

Dr. J. Gordon Melton publishes the first edition of The Vampire Book, a major listing of facts of myths, legends and includes details on the vampire community.

1995 - S.Y. 1 - YEAR OF AWAKENINGS

Within the The Sabretooth Clan:

Working at Limelight at night making fangs Sebastiaan begins his first job making fangs during the day at Andromeda Body Piercing on Saint Marks Place in NYC. Here he expands to working at Halloween Adventure on 4th Avenue NYC during the Halloween season.

August 7th while involved in the "Rennie" community at the New York Renaissance Faire he decides upon the name Sabretooth for his fang business over the "Dark Tooth Fairy." August 17th shortly after founding Sabretooth Sebastiaan meets Victor Magnus at Abracadabra magic shop in Greenwich Village.

That Halloween, at the invite of one of his fang clients Father Sebastiaan attends the legendary Memnoch Ball in New Orleans coordinated by Anne Rice and her fanclub the ARVLFC (Anne Rice Vampire Lestat Fan Club.) This ball was sold out and invite only, over 5000 guests including Kirsten Dunst at Saint Elizabeth's orphanage in the Garden District.

This immediately inspired the creation of the New York Vampyre Ball, which would evolve into the Endless Night events.

1996 - S.Y. 2 - YEAR OF FOUNDATIONS

Within the The Sabretooth Clan:

On January 28th at the Bank nightclub Sebastiaan hosts the first New York Vampyre Ball at the Bank nightclub with Empire Hideous, Voltaire and DJ Erebus (Ian Fford). Over 350 guests attend and it is the bridging event between "old school" and "new school" elements of the New York vampire community.

July 16th reporter Suzan Walsh disappears investigating vampire covens of the East Village, which brings a massive media attention to the NYC vampire community. Sebastiaan is in the center of this media response because of his fang and event business.

Tuesday July 28th club mogul Peter Gatien rents Sabretooth the Limelight for the Vampyre Ball III, the entire club for what to this day is the largest vampire ball to date with 2400 guests. Limelight finally closes from the fallout of pressure from the court case over murderer and drug dealer Michael Alig (see the movie <u>Party Monster</u> for this story).

August of this year Sebastiaan is invited by Chi Chi Valenti to host the party "Long Black Veil and the Vampyre Lounge" to open the following year at the newly opening MOTHER nightclub.

At the Royal Amusements event hosted by latex designer "The Baroness," Sebastiaan meets metal worker PN D'Drennan. They discuss the creation of the now legendary Legacy Ankh. The Vampyre Ball events continue at the Bank the week before Halloween.

Elsewhere in the Vampire World:

Voila Johnston's book <u>Dhampir: Childe of the Blood</u> is published.

Jeff Guinn's <u>Something in the Blood</u> is published.

Konstantinos's book <u>Vampires: The Occult Truth</u> is published.

Vampires appear on Ricki Lake.

April 2, <u>Kindred the Embraced</u> airs on FOX, a TV show produced by Aaron Spelling and inspired by <u>Vampire: The Masquerade</u>.

1997 - S.Y. 3 - YEAR OF THE BLACK VEILS

Within the The Sabretooth Clan:

Long Black Veil (LBV) On Wednesday March 12th the vampire event opens at MOTHER in the seedy Meat Packing district. Within this night the Sabretooth Clan would be formally established.

In July, Master Metal Manipulator D'Drennan delivers Father Sebastiaan the final version of the Legacy Ankh in a wooden coffin. He presents the ankh to writer Raymond T McNally at the Dracula 97: A Centennial Celebration in Los Angeles for his blessings.

In August the Sabretooth Emporium opens at the Halloween Adventure at 104 4th Avenue. It is the world's first full-time fangshop.

On Halloween Sebastiaan attends the Anne Rice Coven Ball in New Orleans. Seeing this one-night event, he decides New Orleans needs a full weekend of events. He begins planning the Endless Night Festival.

Sebastiaan writes the original "Black Veils," the code of conduct for the Long Black Veil night at MOTHER.

Elsewhere in the Vampire World:

Joss Whedon's series Buffy the Vampire Slayer debuts on TV.

Mick Mercer's book The Hex Files: A Gothic Bible is published.

Many vampire lifestyle websites launch the online vampire community (OVC).

1998 - S.Y. 4 - YEAR OF THE ENDLESS NIGHT

Within the The Sabretooth Clan:

TV appearances on MTV and CNN and appearances in Glamour Magazine, Cosmopolitan, the New York Times, New York Time Out, and InStyle Magazines establish a worldwide reputation for Father Sebastiaan and Sabretooth fangs.

People flock from around the world to visit the Sabretooth Emporium at the Halloween Adventure and attend Vampyre Ball and LBV events in New York. The VC in NYC gains world recognition. This summer Sebastiaan invites Anne Rice biographer Katherine Ramsland to host a night at LBV. They begin collaborating on Vampyre Magazine and he writes the first Vampyre Almanac 1997-8 Edition. Hot Topic with a small supplemental ankh, sells 20,000 copies in six weeks, and puts Sabretooth Clan and Endless Night on the map.

September 23rd Katherine Ramsland's book Piercing the Darkness releases. It follows the footsteps of Suzan Walsh's disappearance. Featuring many in the Sabretooth Clan and the New York Vampyre Ball, it helps solidify Sabretooth into history.

This Halloween is the first Endless Night Festival 1 in New Orleans at the Omni Royal Hotel. 600 guests from around the world attend this weekend long event. The first New Orleans Vampyre Ball was held with Empress Chi Chi Valenti and Poppy Z. Brite as a special secret guest. Inkubus Sukkubus a pagan vampyre band from the UK headlines. The concept of the first Endless Night is to create complimentary events since the Anne Rice Coven Ball was only one night.

Elsewhere in the Vampire World:

Joss Whedon's series Buffy the Vampire Slayer is becoming a smash hit. Blade the movie is released bringing attention to the concept of vampire clans and a community within and without the VC.

Anne Rice's books Pandora and The Vampire Armand are published.

1999 - S.Y. 5 - YEAR OF GOTHAM HALO

Within the The Sabretooth Clan:

The Sabretooth Clan is now world renowned and the VC in NYC a full time, in person community with Long Black Veil now weekly at the center of the East Coast VC.

With the rise of the internet and AOL going flat rate per month the vampire scene begins to evolve rapidly and many terms from Sabretooth Clan spread throughout the internet.

The Endless Night moves back to NYC from New Orleans due to an opportunity to be held on Halloween Night at MOTHER.

Elsewhere in the Vampire World:

Anne Rice's book Vittorio the Vampire is published.

House Kheperu announces itself to the world online.

Buffy the Vampire Slayer brings more mainstream attention to vampire culture.

2000 - S.Y. 6 - YEAR OF TRANSFORMATIONS

Within the The Sabretooth Clan:

With the gentrification Meat Packing District on MOTHER's Day, Chi Chi Valenti announces MOTHER will close in June. The last LBV is held on Thursday June 15th and the club closes a week later to many of the alternative community's disappointment. An era ended but LBV moved on to another club right away at True on 23rd St.

Sebastiaan sells the Sabretooth Emporium at the Halloween Adventure Shop to Lestat, one of the LBV DJs who renames it: Transformatorium. On Halloween weekend Endless Night returns to New Orleans and is held at the House of Blues with the Cruxshadows performing.

At this time Sebastiaan is the webmaster for PunishmentSquare.com and the dungeon Pandora's Box in Chelsea. He creates Sanguinarium publishing and publishes the Vampyre Almanac 2000, a full color book.

2001 - S.Y. 7 - YEAR OF THE PHOENIX

Within the The Sabretooth Clan:

Long Black Veil continues at True on 23rd St. in NYC and it gains in popularity. Many other promoters from MOTHER move their events and True becomes the center point of the alternative community in NYC. Empress Chi Chi and Johnny Dynell of MOTHER reopens a sister club "Daddy" on 1st Avenue. Sadly it is short lived and closes quickly as the disasters of 9-11 change the soul of NYC forever.

Endless Night still goes on in New Orleans, even with a short attendance at the Conti Muse Wax Museum.

The New York Vampire Ball "Anti-Valentines Day" takes a break to found and establish the Court of Lazarus on Valentines Day weekend at Jekyll & Hydes in Greenwich village.

2002 - S.Y. 8 - YEAR OF HORIZONS

Within the The Sabretooth Clan:

The Endless Night in New Orleans moves to the beautiful Gallier Hall on Halloween weekend. With a magnificent group of people it is highly successful.

With NYC nightlife and the VC in shambles from 9-11, Sebastiaan relocates to Germany, however soon finds friends in Amsterdam and resides there until January 2005.

2003 - S.Y. 9 - YEAR OF A SECOND AGE

Within the The Sabretooth Clan:

Traveling around Europe, Sebastiaan begins rebuilding the Sabretooth Clan again in his original vision. Germany is not receptive to VC in his vision, yet the Netherlands is more responsive.

Sebastiaan befriends "Kimma," the priest in the Kerk van Satan in Amsterdam. They begin collaboration on a book entitled "V" which will include some of the works of Michelle Belanger (Vampire Codex.) The collaboration of Sebastiaan and Kimma results in the birth of the Ordo Strigoi Vii (OSV,) the esoteric wing of the Sabretooth Clan.

Endless Night in New Orleans moves to the room upstairs at 735 Bourbon St. Although small, it is still a fireball of energy.

The producers of the TV show Mad Mad House contact Sebastiaan in an effort to get assistance on booking people for a reality TV series. Sebastiaan consults and aids in casting Don Henrie, the vampire on the show.

Elsewhere in the Vampire World:

Underworld is released with Kate Beckinsale. Sony Pictures and Screen Gems are sued by White Wolf due to similarities to Vampire: the Masquerade & Werewolf: Apocalypse. The case is settled out of court.

2004 - SY. 10 - YEAR OF REBORN LEGACY

Within the The Sabretooth Clan:

With Sabretooth going strong in Amsterdam, Sebastiaan travels around Europe fanging dozens of people. From Switzerland to France to London to Germany he is networking the Sabretooth Clan like never before. The OSV temple with Kerk van Satan in Amsterdam and the Illuminates of

Thanateros, a chaos magic order.

Instead of hosting the Anti-Valentines Ball in NYC, Sebastiaan produces an Endless Night in Amsterdam, where he meets French journalist Laurant Courau working on a film documentary project called <u>Vampyres: Reality is Stranger than Fiction</u>.

On Halloween, Endless Night takes place in the entire club 735 Bourbon with over 800 guests over 4 days. Highly successful he also releases a hardcover edition of <u>V</u> with Aangel Press of Amsterdam with Kinma as the publisher.

Elsewhere in the Vampire World:

On March 4th the TV show <u>"Mad Mad House"</u> with the Vampire Don Henrie is released, bringing national attention to the VC.

2005 - S.Y. 11 - Year of Broken Hearts

Within the The Sabretooth Clan:

After three years in Europe, Sebastiaan returns to NYC where he and Victor Magnus host the annual Endless Night:Anti-Valentines Vampire Ball at Rare. Outside he meets Jeniviva, who would become a major influence on the Sabretooth Clan and Endless Night events.

While in Florida visiting friends, Sebastiaan learns D'Drennan, the artist who designed the Vampire Legacy Ankh had committed suicide on Valentines Day. Immediately Sebastiaan returns to NYC. D'Drennan's funeral was a traumatic event for the Sabretooth Clan and the Legacy. The entire VC of NYC gathers at True on 23rd St. to celebrate his life, with speakers and performers.

Back living in NYC and taking over the Fangshop at the Halloween Adventure, Sebastiaan settles in and begins working more with Victor Magnus at Club Avalon, in the old Limelight space running a party called Church.

On August 29th Hurricane Katrina made landfall in New Orleans, displacing many and ending Halloween. The Endless Night is relocated to NYC and takes place at a club on the Bowery called Crash Mansion.

The Vampyre Almanac becomes VampyreAlmanac.com and is the largest active Vampire community online.

Elsewhere in the Vampire World:

Twilight by Stephanie Meyer is published.

2006 - S.Y. 12 - YEAR OF REFLECTIONS

Within the The Sabretooth Clan:

Black Abby opens at Uncle Mings with Victor Magnus in NYC.

Endless Night takes place in NYC.

2007 - SY. 13 - YEAR OF THE RETURNING

Within the The Sabretooth Clan:

Anti-Valentines Ball in NYC at Element (The Bank) in February.

June – Sebastiaan moves to Paris with Sacar Mina.

October – Endless Night returns to New Orleans at Conti Muse Wax Museum with Voltaire.

Chad Savage, Bloody Mary and Sebastiaan give vision to Fred Samedi, the mascot of the Endless Night events.

Elsewhere in the Vampire World:

"Moonlight" TV series premiers.

2008 - S.Y. 14 - YEAR OF THE UNDEAD

Within the The Sabretooth Clan:

Endless Night: New Orleans Vampire Ball returns to the House of Blues

"Day of the Dead."

Elsewhere in the Vampire World:

True Blood premieres on HBO.

Bathory a film about Elizabeth Bathory is released.

2009 - S.Y. 15 - RETURN TO VERSAILLES

Within the The Sabretooth Clan:

Endless Night: New Orleans Vampire Ball returns to the House of Blues "A Night at Versailles."

The Sanguinomicon is released on Lulu.com in four editions.

Elsewhere in the Vampire World:

The Strain, a book by Guillermo Del Toro and Chuck Hogan, is published.

2010 - S.Y. 16 - YEAR OF MASQUES

Within the The Sabretooth Clan:

Endless Night: New Orleans Vampire Ball returns to the House of Blues "Lucifer's Masquerade."

Sanguinomicon : Lexicon of the Living Vampire is published by Wesier Books.

2011 - S.Y. 17 - YEAR OF ENTROPY

Within the The Sabretooth Clan:

Endless Night: New Orleans Vampire Ball returns to the House of Blues "Steampunk Soiree."

November 19th, Endless Night belly dancer and Sabretooth member Jeniviva dies in a car accident.

2012 - S.Y. 18 - Year of Changing Veils

Within the The Sabretooth Clan:

Endless Night: New Orleans Vampire Ball returns to the House of Blues "C'thulhu Apocalypse."

<u>Vampyre Magick : Grimoire of the Living Vampire</u> is published by Wesier Books.

2013 - S.Y. 19 - Year of Omens

Within the The Sabretooth Clan:

Endless Night: New Orleans Vampire Ball returns to the House of Blues "Zompire."

2014 - S.Y. 20 - Year of Victoriental Dreams

Feb. - Denver Vampire Ball with Isibella Karnstein is attended by Father Sebastiaan.

Within the The Sabretooth Clan:

Endless Night: New Orleans Vampire Ball returns to the House of Blues "Victoriental."

Elsewhere in the Vampire World:

Anne Rice's book <u>Prince Lestat</u> is published and Anne Rice returns to New Orleans.

2015 - S.Y. 21 - Year of Penny Dreadfuls

Within the The Sabretooth Clan:

On Halloween night proper the Endless Night: New Orleans Vampire Ball returns to the House of Blues "Penny Dreadfuls."

Vice Magazine <u>The Real True Blood</u> released on February 9th.

Feb. 15th the Endless Night: New York Vampire Ball Anti-Valentines takes place at Jekyll & Hyde Club on Times Square

Feb. 28th the first Endless Night: Tampa Vampire Ball at the Castle Ybor City in Florida.

2016 - S.Y. 22 - YEAR OF THE CIRQUE

Within the The Sabretooth Clan:

Endless Night: New Orleans Vampire Ball "Cirque du Vampyre" at The House of Blues at 225 Decatur St.. in New Orleans.

2017 - S.Y. 23 - YEAR OF GODS & MONSTERS

On Halloween Endless Night Festival "Gods & Monsters" takes place at the House of Blues in New Orleans.

First Endless Night: Los Angeles Vampire Ball at the Globe Theatre on Sunday February 19th.

FATHER SEBASTIAAN'S

ENDLESS NIGHT
VAMPIRE BALL PRESENTS

WWW.ENDLESSNIGHT.COM
#ENDLESSNIGHTVAMPIREBALL
FACEBOOK.COM/ENDLESSNIGHTVAMPIREBALL
INSTAGRAM.COM/ENDLESSNIGHTVB

Vampire MUSES

OVERVIEW

FThe Vampire Muses of Father Sebastiaan's Endless Nights are exceptional members of the Sabretooth Clan and Vampire World. The concept of Vampire Muses is inspired by the glamour and seductiveness of pinups and dandies, and celebrates the fierce, strong, and driven fanged ladies and gents who embody the Black Veils of Elegant, Empowering, Magical, Mysterious, Primal, Romantic, and Seductive. There is no nudity involved or required for Vampire Muses, only glamour, beauty, a strong will and presence, and the support of the Vampire Current of the Sabretooth Clan. Some reciepients of the Muses Awards include models La Esmeralda of Germany, Morgan Kay of Belgium, Lea DeCountessa of Paris and, Ophelia Overdose of Germany.

Being awarded the title of Vampire Muse is an opportunity that opens other doors, including appearances at Endless Night Vampire balls, possible modeling contracts, and appearances at horror, fantasy, and science fiction conventions.

To be considered for the title of Vampire Muse, you must be a prospective or current fang client of Father Sebastiaan. Before applying, please go to FatherSebastiaan.com and learn about Father Sebastiaan's fangsmithing business, and review the photo sets of past Vampire Muses. You are also strongly encouraged to read the books "Black Veils: The Vampire Lexicon", and "The Vampire Sebastiaan: Vampire World History" for a better understanding of the philosophy behind the culture of the Sabretooth Clan. After that research, your application must include a short statement as to why you are interested in the title of Vampire Muse, your location, and at least ten tasteful photos from your modeling portfolio.

VAMPIRE MUSES

THREONDY IN VELVET
LONDON UK

ENDLESS NIGHT
VAMPIRE
MUSES

LA DUTCHESSA
AMSTERDAM
PHOTO: VIONA ART

ENDLESS NIGHT

VAMPIRE MUSES

EMMA VAUXDEVIL
HOUSTON TEXAS
PHOTO: DMRDEPICTIONS

LEA CONTESSA
PARIS

ENDL... VAMPIRE MUSES

ENDLESS NIGHT
VAMPIRE MUSES

DANI DIVINE
LONDON UK

LA ESMERALDA
GERMANY

ENDLESS NIGHT
VAMPIRE
MUSES

ENDLESS NIGHT
VAMPIRE
MUSES
XIOMORA
PHILADELPHIA

ENDLESS NIGHT
VAMPIRE
MUSES

MAHAFSOUN
VAMPIRE QUEEN OF
VANCOUVER

PHOTO: LILIAN LIU HEADRESS: NIGEL CROW

Show Your Support

I. Gift A copy of Black Veils
Order a copy of Black Veils for a friend who is interested in Vampire Culture for their birthday or a special occasion.

II. Post your Vampire Family Signal
Post a picture of your book on Instagram and other social media channels with the hashtags #Black Veils and #VampireCulture. Look at other photos that other readers have posted and get creative. Suggested mode is to post picture of Black Veils on your altar. Don't forget to add the link www.vampireworld.com/blackveils or the direct link to Black Veils on Amazon.com.

III. Suggest a Black Veil
Contact the publisher via email and suggest ideas for a new Black Veil that has not been covered yet.

IV. Readings of the Veils
Like a poetry reading, record a video of reading out loud your favorite or relevant Black Veils, and share it on YouTube or at an event.

Vampire Courts
a vampire salon noir

A "Vampire Court" is known within the Vampire Culture (VC) as a private gathering held for members in a specific geographic region or for a set purpose. Courtly events are different from Vampire Balls in that they are more intimate events "hidden in plain sight" close to the profane Dayside World and set certain standards of entry to focus the spirit and energy of the gathering. "Outer Courts" are semi-public events with standards of dress code, while "Inner Courts" are more private and invite only by the Host. Courts can be held as one-off special events, annually, bimonthly, quarterly or monthly.

The term "Court" hails from the romanticism of the Vampire Mythos and are about fellowship, ceremony, and creating a sacred space where individuals are free to be themselves in the Nightside. Within the "Old School" Sanguinarium model, Courts were inspired by the Salon Noir esoteric and poetic gatherings of 19th century La Belle Époque Paris. Andy Warhol's "FACTORY" is an example of a modern artistic court. A true court should hold up to the standards set forth in the Black Veils of Family, Romance, Class, Elegance, Ceremony, Seduction, Mystery, Secrets, Ritual, Magic, Nobility and Community.

One major misconception is that a court "is" a group or organization, yet in historical reality a court is "held" as an event / gathering of community influencers or descriptive of a physical place. Titles within a court are akin to Freemason and titles are only active when court is in session and require functionally active actual duties, not obscure positions of false power over others. The first official Vampire Court was "The Court of Gotham" NYC in 1997, founded as a cocktail party and meet up outside the Long Black Veil events where members of the VC could talk and socialize without loud music.

Traditionally an old school Sanguinarium "formal court" contains the following elements:

THE HOST(s) is the lead officer(s) of a Court. For more theatrical courts Hosts can go by glamorous noble or royal formal titles such as Impresario, Magister / Magistra, Regent, Comte / Comtessa, King / Queen, etc.

COMPERE is the "master of ceremonies" to make announcements and address the court. This can often be the Host or larger more organized gatherings be its own position.

DIRECTOR (formerly called "Vizier") is in charge of hospitality and operations. Duties include setting up the court and overseeing the staff.

COURTIERS or "citizens" are those who are formal "card carrying" members of the court.

RITUALS are often held such as a Red Mass, communion, banishings, naming ceremonies, consecrations, etc. involving members of the community who are spiritually minded. Sometimes a "Hierophant" is appointed to oversee the rituals.

READINGS of poetry, literature, Black Veils, etc. will add a flair of class and sophistication.

DRESS CODE is usually formal attire, top hats, corsets, vampire or all black is very common for a "witches sabbath" vibe.

CHARITIES or fundraisers are often held to raise money for the court or a charity the court is fond of.

FANGSMITHS are usually endorsed by the court and serve the members of the court.

SIGIL of the court is often a royal / noble crest based on ancient nobility and worn as lapel pins or a "Voodoo Veve."

PERFORMANCES are usually held including burlesque acts, belly dancers, illusionists, etc.

MYSTICS such as a tarot reader and other forms of divination are usually set up to read within the court.

MUSIC is usually held in the dark, ambient, ritualistic, classical, gothic genres by guest or resident DJs.

GATEKEEPER is the master of security, enforces the dress code and holds the guest list.

PRESENTATION of a discussion circle on a particular topic ranging from energy work to social dynamics to ancient languages.

BANQUET should be held right after opening. Food is a powerful element of bringing people together. It can be catered or pot luck.

BDSM should be kept to light sensual play such as shibari; never outrageous or vulgar.

LOCATION should be a decadent salon lounge or beautiful suite in a luxurious hotel. AirBnB offers great options. Should be secure and secluded from the mundane world.

A WARNING: Have fun and be theatrical, don't take things too seriously, enjoy the glamour and beauty of the Vampire Mythos and lifestyle.

Example court agenda:

8pm - Gathering begins, social time
9pm - Dinner
10pm - Discussion Circle
11pm - Ceremonies
12pm - Party : Dancing, BDSM play, etc.

long black veil

(new york's historical vampire haven)

By VICTOR MAGNUS

The remarkable Long Black Veil or "LBV" events truly hold a unique place in the history of New York City's nightlife. LBV began in 1997 as "Long Black Veil & The Vampyre Lounge" on the second Wednesday of each month at the legendary MOTHER nightclub on 14th and Washington Streets in New York City's meat-packing district. Chi Chi Valenti, also known as 'The Empress,' one of the owners of MOTHER, and her life mate, the famous DJ Johnny Dynell, conceived and named the event after hearing the mournful song "Long Black Veil."

The song "Long Black Veil" was written in the late 1950s by Nashville songwriters Marijohn Wilkin and Danny Dill, who were inspired by newspaper accounts of two non-related events: the real life murder case of a New Jersey priest and reports of a mysterious woman in a black veil who regularly visited silent movies star Rudolph Valentino's grave. Primarily associated with Johnny Cash, the song has also been covered by many artists including Lefty Frizell (the original singer), The Band, Joan Baez, Nick Cave, and the Dave Mathews Band. However, it was the 1995 version of the song recorded by the Celtic/Irish traditional music

LONG BLACK VEIL - Uncovering the Legend by Victor Magnus

875 Washington St. & West 14th St. NYC

LONG BLACK VEIL
new york city
@
MOTHER
www.longblackveil.com   www.mothernyc.com
ANCIENT CULTURES

Impressed by already existing and popular MOTHER events such as Jackie 60 (Tuesdays) and Click+ Drag (Saturdays), Father Sebastiaan insisted that the same "template" of these other events also be used for LBV. This template for success relied on décor, an exclusive door policy with a strict dress code, stage performances every week, and the magickal energies of the MOTHER venue itself. DJs Ian Fford, Lestat, and Johanna Constantine presided over the early dance floors. Initially, the main attendees were the clients of Sebastiaan and this core element formed the foundation of what became known as "Clan Sabretooth."

In less than a year LBV's success demanded that it become a weekly Sunday event at MOTHER, with the addition of host and doorman or "Gatekeeper" Father Vincent under the name temporary Fang Club Gotham. This short-lived name change was intended to unite NYC's Vampire Culture with the Fang Club in Hollywood, which was owned by Jack Dean Strauss. 1997 also marked the year that DJ Jason of Alchemy became the host DJ in the Vampyre Lounge within LBV held in Versailles room of MOTHER.

Also in 1997, Anne Rice's biographer Katherine Ramsland contacted Father Sebastiaan and asked him to serve as a consultant for a book she was writing entitled Piercing the Darkness: Undercover with Vampires in America Today. Ramsland's intention was to follow in the last known footsteps of investigative reporter Susan Walsh, who disappeared around the same time as the historic Vampyre Ball at the Limelight in July 1996. A release party for the book was held at LBV in 1998, where Ms. Ramsland read excerpts and signed copies for the attendees.

Alchemistress Ambrosia, Creator of the Bloodbath Cocktail

1998 also saw the release of the first printed edition of <u>Vampyre Almanac</u> and the original Legacy Ankh pendants. These Ankhs were sold around the world through alternative retail outlets such as Hot Topic. The worldwide release of <u>Vampyre Almanac</u> and <u>Piercing the Darkness</u> brought international attention to the culture and to the name "Long Black Veil." That year LBV took up its traditional place on Thursday evenings at MOTHER, where it remained until the final days of the club in June 2000.

During this "golden age" of the vampyre scene in Gotham, many legendary events such as 1999's Endless Night Festival, the annual Lost Boys' Beach Party, The Anti-Valentine's Ball and the fetish/body arts Xorvia events were spawned. Guests who entered the gates of MOTHER included celebrities like Debbie Harry (Blondie) and fangsmiths including Dnash and Maven of Dark Awakenings.

The most important legacy of LBV is that it was at that event that the original "Vampyre code of ethics" was introduced. Inspired by the structure employed by the Fetish/BDSM subcultures and renaissance faire etiquette, this code became known as "The Black Veils." Originally developed as the house rules of LBV, this code of ethics is now accepted worldwide and is the standard code of vampyre/Vampire culture.

"The Black Veils" code was revised in 2002 by Michelle Belanger of House Kheperu from Ohio, and it has even found its way into mainstream popular culture in episodes of C.S.I. Las Vegas and mentioned as a "sacred script" by Don Henrie on the Sci-Fi Channel's reality show Mad, Mad House.

Another lasting Legacy of LBV is the Bloodbath cocktail. Created by the resident bartending mixologist of LBV, the Alchemistress Ambrosia, the Bloodbath is now the most popular drink enjoyed by VC all around the world. SEE Bloodbath Black Veil.

With the closing of MOTHER in the year 2000, Father Sebastiaan chose to continue the event by relocating to True nightclub on West 23rd Street, near Broadway in Manhattan. LBV remained there for two more years until he decided to end this event in the spring of 2002 in favor of throwing future reunion parties instead.

LBV had a lasting impression and it resonated in the minds of many in the VC throughout the Gotham Halo (New York City area), North America, and the world.

Teaming up with NYC events promoter Master Steelow (who began his career as a go-go boy at Long Black Veil) Father Sebastiaan promoted a series of reunion LBV parties at Flamingo East nightclub on 2nd Avenue and 14th Street in Manhattan starting in the fall of 2002. When Sebastiaan moved to Europe in the fall of 2002, he hosted the last LBV reunion for almost a year.

Throughout LBV's history, knowledge of the event has spread into mainstream consciousness, through various media outlets such as Glamour, Cosmopolitan, In-Style, The New York Times, Time

Out New York, The book Piercing the Darkness, and on television's History Channel, The Learning Channel, Travel Channel, and many others. Even with this exposure, LBV has managed to maintain its true underground integrity through strict media policies against exploitation and sensationalism of the Vampire, fetish and gothic communities.

Long Black Veil has inspired many other NYC vampire events including Court of Lazarus, Black Abbey, Black Invokation, Hidden Shadow's Realm of Darkness, The Court of Gotham, and the many noir havens throughout the world including Black Atlantis (Atlanta), Black Sunset (Miami), Black Trillium (Toronto), Black Xion (Amsterdam), and many others.

Father Sebastiaan and the Legacy team will continue working hard to provide first class events for the Vampyre/Vampire community under the veil of Endless Night / Vampire World, by keeping standards high and providing this dark subculture many forms of quality events and media for many years to come.

ABOUT THE AUTHOR: Victor Magnus is a senior member of Sabretooth Clan (Brood of 1995) and has been an active member on and off over the years. Today he is the GateKeeper of the Endless Night Vampire Ball events in New York and New Orleans.

Requiem Veils
(the Risen)

The Risen are many souls of the Family who are no longer incarnated but who have contributed greatly to the Legacy. Two in particular are significant in our collective story: P.N. D'Drennan (creator of the Legacy Ankh) and Jeniviva (the premiere performer of Endless Night Vampire Ball events from 2005 to 2011). We immortalize them here in the Legacy with their own Black Veils so future Vampire generations will know their names and stories.

PN D'Drennan

(master metal manipulator)

(born ? - D: February 14th 2005)

Master Metal Manipulator PN D'Drennan is a historical personality associated with the New York Vampire Community (Gotham Halo,) and loved by all who met him. He is best known as the artist that in September 1996 Father Sebastiaan commissioned to design the Legacy Ankh, the symbol of the Black Veils and the Legacy. He once said he had a "demon's hand" helping him craft his artifacts. A true gentleman, the symbolism of his metal creations helped to define the early days of the VC of Gotham Halo. He was often seen attending many NYC events such as Long Black Veil, The Bank, the Vampire Ball, Click + Drag and many other events at MOTHER. Sadly he passed away on February 14th 2005 leaving the Legacy of his precious metal artifacts behind. We honor his memory as a Black Veil so those who loved him or never knew him can hold him in their thoughts and hearts.

Photo by Jana Marcus

Jeniviva
(endless night performer)
(April 9 1975 - November 19th 2011)

Hailing from Gotham Halo (New York City) Jeniviva Mai was the central Endless Night performer from 2005 to 2011 in New Orleans, Paris, Florida and New York. She was known as a mother, friend and free spirit who guided the Current. She maintained friendships and relationships that were lifelong and effected many of the Family and our Black Swans with a divine sense. Jeni graced the stage of the Endless Night: Paris Vampire Ball 2011 at the La machine du Moulin Rouge in her most magnificent performance, followed by Endless Night New Orleans 2011. She was known for her beauty and incredible sense of humor, inspiring young dancers and establishing the long tradition of bellydance, burlesque, and theatrical dance at Endless Night which lasts until this day.

Black Veils
WHEEL OF THE YEAR

Nightside Festival
Dec. 21 N. Hemisphere
Jun. 21 S. Hemisphere

Halloween
Samhain
Oct.30-Nov.1

Crimson Festival
Saint Valentines
February 14

Rising Festival
Sept. 21-24

Black Veil Fest
March 15

Bast Festival
Wild Hunt
August 7

Walpurgisnacht
"Dragon Festival / Beltaine
May 1

Dayside Festival
June 21 N. Hemisphere
Dec. 21 S. Hemisphere

Black Veils

COMING FORTH BY NIGHT - PREVIEW

the Current

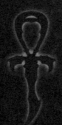

the Current

The Current refers to the group spirit of the Sabretooth Clan, which can also be seen as a living entity that is the result of the Family's agreement, rituals, actions, traditions, philosophy and culture. The Current is often referred to as the psychological and/or spiritual "Blood" of the Family, as it is what binds the Sabretooths together. The Current is not physical. Rather it is made up of subtle energies such as thoughts, emotions, ideas, concepts and links.

As the Current flows from the success and personal evolution of each individual Sabretooth, it is added to the collective flow of energy within the Family, which can then in turn be tapped by members. The quality and quantity of individuals in agreement is a resource that amplifies the Current as a whole, as long as the individuals make the sincere effort to invest their passion, love and loyalty. As an egregore, the Current is an elemental built from psychological, spiritual, cultural and philosophical ties and is fueled by agreement, offerings, collective actions and recognition. Egregores can be born, forgotten and evolve. Ancient examples of egregores can even be personified as deities or heroes, entire cultures, and even living stories, mythologies and legends. Modern examples of egregores can be the "team spirit" of a sports team, interactions between the fans of a superhero or TV series (like Dr. Who or Star Wars), or the collective consciousness of a corporation such as Google, Tesla or Apple.

The Current can be felt as the vibe of the Endless Night events. Every time an individual goes through the Rites of Transformation they empower the Current by feeling the excitement so many others have felt before them when looking in the mirror with their fangs for the first time. The Current is invoked and amplified within each individual Sabretooth's awakening and interactions, and empowered through Quest, agreement and application of our traditions and actions. The Current is a living, breathing entity with its own dharma, karma, personality, and agenda, strengthened through the Family. "Pulses" are aspects and focuses of the Current and focus on different Black Veils including Ramhkt (Magic, Ritual, Knowledge, Dreams and Secrets), Kitra (Witch, Seduction, Sensuality and Romance) and Mradu (Chivalry, Love, Warrior and Honour). The Current is the soul of our Legacy and the Sabretooth Clan.

Pulses

ULSES within the Sabretooth Clan help members of the Family to focus on specific BlackVeils. They each represent a different archetype within the Current. There are five major Pulses including Kitra (Lovers). Mradu (Warriors). Ramkht (Magicians). Samedi (Hosts). and Elorath (Dragons).

KITRA (Lovers) focus on the Black Veils of Dance, Libertine, Romance, Seduction, and Witch. They are the weavers and councilors of the Current.

MRADU (Warriors) focus on the Black Veils of Chivalry, Honor, Love, Loyalty, Nobility, and Warrior. They are the guardians and protectors of the Current.

RAMKHT (Magicians) focus on the Black Veils of Creativity, Dreaming, Knowledge, Magic, and Wisdom. They are the inspiration and directors of the Current.

SAMEDI (Hosts) focus on the Black Veils of Absinthe, Decadance, Hospitality, Humor, Music and Rock & Roll. They are the Acolytes of Fred Samedi, the guardian spirit of the Endless Night events.

ELORATH (Dragons) focus on the Black Veils of Apotheosis, Dragon, Immortality, Mastery, and Sorcery. Initiates of this Pulse are the Priesthood of the Current.

Kitra
"the lovers"

itra, "The Crowned Ones" or "the Lovers" is the Pulse of the Current that represents the Black Veils of Witch, Sensuality, Seduction, Emotion, Dance, Music, Art, Elegance, Glamour, Creativity, and Passion. Kitra are weavers of life and the matriarchal aspect of the Current. The Pulse of Kitra is often associated with the goddesses Lilith, Kali, Aphrodite, Isis, and Hecate. Deeply rooted in feminine energy and chivalry, the Kitra are very sensual and sexually libertine, yet predatory, also containing healing energy specific to Vampires. They are councilors and advisors. Those attuned to the Pulse of Kitra can be very assertive and resourceful and often act as the conscience of the Family.

Kitra energy inspires an intense need to give love to and nurture others. When Kitra manifests as avatar in the mind, rituals or visions, she most often appears during the full moon as a beautiful nightklad maiden wearing a silver crown or Hindu-style headdress. She may have long black or silver hair, violet eyes, and be accompanied by great cats of varying types. Kitra garb is very tribal and loves bells, feathers, and long flowing garments and crowns.

While the Pulse of Kitra is primarily associated with the female gender, masculine identifying individuals who are attuned to her current are known as ASZURES. They may adopt a dandy-like appearance and be very beautiful and elegant, yet masculine in energy. Examples of those attuned to Kitra include the temple maidens of the Second Temple in Jerusalem, the Maenads or the female worshippers of Dionysus, and the priestesses of Isis in Ancient Egypt and Greece. Kitra is related to the Empress and High Priestess cards of the Greater Arcana in the Tarot.

KITRA "THE LOVER"

Mradu
"the Warriors"

radu is the Warrior Pulse of the Current and represents the Black Veils of Knight, Warrior, Chivalry, Honor, Love, Loyalty and Nobility. Those attuned to Mradu energy find themselves embracing loyalty, grounded energy and love. The Mradu is more tied to the corporeal reality than the other Pulses. Mradu is equated with the currents of the patriarchal gods of ancient times such as Zeus, Thor, Brahma, Jupiter, Osiris, Cernunnos, and Mithras.

The energy of Mradu is that of a chivalrous knight who never breaks their word and maintains a strong code of honor. A deep, yet often hidden need to be loved makes Mradu extremely passionate, charming, and gregarious. Mradu has a slowly kindled yet intense temper and, due to their intense loyalty, holds powerful grudges against those seen as betrayers. Once a member of the Mradu Pulse bonds with someone, they are intensely dedicated and loyal to that individual.

While the Pulse of Mradu is commonly associated with the male gender, there are a number of female identifying individuals attuned to this Pulse. Those attuned to Mradu energy will often have strong Corporeal bodies, being broad-shouldered and muscular with a sturdy immune system. The Pulse of Mradu magically can be called upon to aid in grounding, banishing, shielding, filtering, and setting up protective and defensive wards. Mradu vestments are very military-like, often incorporating armor, military fatigues, Asian martial arts clothing, and various uniforms. The symbol of Mradu is the blade in its various forms and his totem animal is the lion. Mradu are related to the Strength and Justice cards of the Greater Arcana in the Tarot.

MRADU "THE WARRIOR"

Ramkht
"the Magicians"

amkht, "The Magicians," are the Pulse of the Current which embodies the Black Veils of Magic, Ritual, Dreams, Mastery, Inspiration and Will. Unlike those attuned to the Pulses of Mradu and Kitra, the initiates of the Ramkht are equally likely to be equally male or female in gender. Ramkht energy is often related to deities such as Thoth, Hermes, Vishnu, Artemis, Ixchel, and Brigid.

Ramkht energy is attuned with inspiration and the Will to bring dreams into reality. This makes those attuned to Ramkht well suited for leading rituals, performing scholarly work, and undertaking creative endeavors. The personality of Ramkht is often very serious with a narcissistic bent, yet with a hidden reserve of humor. Ramkht spirits often manifest in visions and dreams in the form of a beautiful androgynous being with luminous skin, pitch black or pearl-white eyes, and long scholarly robes mixed with the vestments of a pharaoh. Those attuned to the Pulse of Ramkht are highly focused in lucid dreaming, OBE (astral projection), meditation, communing with spirits, and accessing the Akashic Records.

The realm most associated with the Pulse of Ramkht is that of dreams and the mistress of abstract thoughts. The tool of Ramkht is the rod or wand used to direct intent. Its vestments are long academic robes or priestly attire. The totem animals of Ramkht are the birds of prey such as the owl, which is also associated with wisdom; and the snake, which is associated with wisdom, language, and healing. The Pulse of Ramkht is related to the Magician and Hierophant cards of the Greater Arcana in the Tarot.

SABRETOOTH CLAN

RAMKHT "THE MAGICIAN"

About the author

Father Sebastiaan is one of the central personalities of the Vampire Culture and community (VC) worldwide. He entered the subculture in 1992, and is known as the the Endless Night Vampire Ball Impresario, author of several books including BLACK VEILS and "Founding Father" of the Sabretooth Clan. He is an avid student of chaos magick, lover of roleplaying games, BDSM educator, student of the paranormal, an expert on Vampire Culture, fascinated by ancient cultures and devoted to exploring art, music, tradition and history.

Over the three decades in the VC, Father has appeared on a multitude of television programs and networks including A&E, CNN, Discovery Channel, History Channel, National Geographic, USA Up All Night, and MTV's Oddville. He was also featured as a central character in the French documentary and book Vampyres: Reality is Stranger than Fiction by Laurent Courau, as well as Katherine Ramsland, Anne Rice biographer's book Piercing the Darkness: Undercover with Vampires in America Today. In print media he and his projects have had feature articles in Cosmopolitan, The New York Times, The Financial Times, InStyle Magazine, Glamour, Skin Two, and New York Time Out.

Sebastiaan was born in San Diego California, grew up in the New York metropolitan area and has lived in Amsterdam, Philadelphia, Los Angeles, Paris, Dubai and Berlin. He now is pursuing his writing career as a gypsy somewhere in the Vampire World.

For more information on Father and his projects please visit www.fathersebastiaan.com.

legacy Ankh

The Legacy Ankh is the sigilium which represents Black Veils, the teachings, culture and philosophy of the Sabretooth Clan. This precious artifact is proudly worn discretely in public and openly in ceremony) by Vampires and Black Swans to symbolize their support and dedication to the Legacy.

In 1996, Master Metal Manipulator Drennan was commissioned by Father Sebastiaan to make an exclusive version of a bladed ankh to represent the Black Veils and the Legacy. Thus was born the Legacy Ankh, the most recognized international symbol of Black Veils and the Legacy. Since there are so many imitators, the Legacy Ankh is legally copyrighted and trademarked by the Sabretooth Clan in order to protect it and to avoid any misuse of the symbol. We wish to make it clear that this particular scimitar-bladed ankh is the exclusive intellectual property of the Sabretooth Clan, and should be recognized and respected as such.

Colored stones in a Legacy Ankh represent how much time has passed since the wearer's Rites of Transformation. Red is for a year and a day, Purple for Five Years and a day and Black for 13+ years.

Related Black Veils : STONE and ANKH.

Legacy Ankh Designs

FLASH ART
CIRCA 2008

A'EDITION
CIRCA 2003

ORIGINAL
D'EDITION
CIRCA 1997

CONCEPT ART
BY D'DRENNAN
CIRCA 1996

B'EDITION
CIRCA 2015

Suggested Reading

General Reading

Power of Myth by Joseph Campbell

Personal Empowerment

Art of Seduction by Robert Greene
Mastery by Robert Greene
The Rules of the Game by Neil Strauss
The 50th Law by Robert Greene and 50 Cent
48 Laws of Power by Robert Greene
33 Strategies of War by Robert Greene
Your Beauty Mark : The Ultimate Guide to Eccentric Glamour by Dita von Teese
The Art of War by Sun Szu
Beyond Good and Evil by Friedrich Nietzsche
Thus Spoke Zarathurstra by Friedrich Nietzsche
How to Win Friends and Influence People by Dale Carnegie

Esoterica / Occult

Lord of the Left Hand Path by Stephen E. Flowers Ph.D.
Satanic Bible by Anton Szandor LaVey
The Satanic Witch by Anton Szandor LaVey
Liber Null & Psychonaut by Peter J. Caroll
The New Enyclopedia of the Occult by John Michael Greer
MONSTERS by John Michael Greer
The Grimoire of Deharan Magick: Kaimana (2005) by Storm Constantine

Essential "Real" Vampire Books

Psychic Vampire Codex by Michelle Belanger
Vampires the Occult Truth by Konstantinos
The Asetian Bible by Luis Marquis
The Vampire Bibles by Nemo / TOV

Fiction

The Vampire Chronicles by Anne Rice
Lost Souls by Poppy Z. Brite
Vampire the Masquerade by Mark Rein-Hagan

Epilogue

Now that you have finished with the Black Veils and are more familiar with the Legacy and the Vampire World, you might think that while we take ourselves very seriously, we at the same time love to live, love and celebrate. Then you are absolutely right! The Sabretooth Clan is a tribe and culture unlike any other within the Vampire World with its own unique ceremonies, rituals, philosophy and traditions. So we hope to one day see you Sitting in the fang throne or maybe joining us at one of the Endless Night Vampire Ball events. But remember, there is but one life that we can improve upon and make the most of!

Don't just survive, thrive!

living vampire
Real Vampire Glossary
by father sebastiaan

This is the terminology most commonly used terms within the "VC" or "Vampire Culture". Please check out the Living / Real Vampire FAQ as a companion to this glossary. This is by no means a definitive glossary.

Ambient Feeding - The most basic of all energy feeding techniques. Feeding on the cloud of lifeforce energy radiated by humans.

Ambient Energy - Excess life force energy radiated from the human body in a cloud. Usually in large groups of people such as sporting events, public streets, cities, public transportation during rush hour, etc.

Aura - The outer layers of the human subtle body, equivalent of the skin.

Awakening - The actual realization of a vampire that recognizes the "Need" and or a strong draw to the vampire archetype.

Astral - a more formal term for the subtle reality, spirit world or "otherside."

Black Swan - A mundane who is friendly to vampire culture and sometimes act as donors.

Black Veils - The teachings, traditions and philosophies of the Sabretooth Clan put into words of power.

Blood and Roses - A vampire wedding or handfasting involving three levels or "rings." "First Rings" is a year and a day, "Second Rings" lasts for 7 years and Third Rings are for eternity. At the end of the duration of each set of rings the couple can renew at that level, let it expire or move to the next level.

Chakras - Energy centers within the subtle body. Some consider them akin to organs.

Communion - To cycle and exchange energy between to two or more energy sensitive vampires.

Coming Out of the Coffin - To publicly acknowledge one is a vampire to friends and family, being open about one's nature. Akin to "Coming out of the Closet" for the LBGT community.

Coven - An immediate family of vampires. (Also check "House".)

Court - A private (closed) or public (outer) event similar to a "salon noir" geographically based gathering of vampires private from the mundane world. Courts are usually formal events which are akin to "salon noir" events of La Belle Epoque France including ceremonies and rituals, dress code (often all black clothing with fangs), live performances, etc.

Dayside - The mundane and profane world of the 5 senses and includes birth/blood family, reason, logic, science, etc.

Deep energy - AKA "core energy" is the deepest part of the individual's subtle body.

Deep feeding - To feed upon the core elements of an individual's life-force

Dharma - Different from fate or destiny this refers to "purpose."

Donors - Non-vampires who willingly "donate" blood or lifeforce energy consensually to vampires especially when deep feeding.

Elder - A senior member of the vampire community who has been around for a long time (usually 5 years) and is often seen as a mentor and leader.

Emotional Vampire - "Emo-vamps" are usually unawakened vampires or individuals who raises emotions is often considered a form of parasitic vampirism. This is described as "traditional psychic vampires" by Anton LaVey in theSatanic Bible and in Psychic Self Defence by Dion Fortune.

Fangdom - The fandom part of the vampire subculture who are fans of TV shows, literature and media such as Twilight fans, Anne Rice fans, etc.

Fangsmith - A craftsperson who makes custom made fangs for the vampire community.

Feeding - The process of gathering or harvesting the excess life-force generated by the human body. The benefits of this include sating the energetic Need and feeding it increases energy inside of us which can be applied for magick and energy work techniques.

Fledgling - A newly awakened vampire, usually within a year of their formal awakening.

Gaja - An individual who takes the lifestyle way too seriously. Often claiming they are truly immortal, dress in outrageous costumes, etc.

Haven - A nightclub, gathering place or event friendly to the vampire subculture.

Halo - The energy signature and "spirit" of a specific geographic area originally founded within the Sabretooth Clan but used by many in the vampire subculture. Examples include "Gotham Halo" is NYC's five boroughs, Westchester, Long Island and NorthEastern NJ, "Angel Halo" is Los Angeles and "Lutetia Halo" is Paris France.

House - A coven of vampires.

Hunters - Ridiculous individuals who think they are actually hunting real vampires. This is usually a myth within the vampire community.

Hybrid - A living vampire who is a mixture of sanguine (blood) and psychic (energy).

Legends - Mundane myths and legends of history outside the Legacy about vampires, including HighGate Cemetery, Dracula, Bathory, etc.

Life-Force - Is also known as prana, chi, ki, etc. and is the energy which animates and radiates from all living beings.

Lifestylers - "Fashion vampires" are individuals who incorporate the vampire archetype into their lifestyle as a philosophy, aesthetic fashion sense (fangs, contacts, clothing) of identity.

Living Vampire - An individual who identifies with the vampire archetype in some way. Also known as a "real vampire."

Long Black Veil - (LBV) was a weekly vampire nightclub in NYC at MOTHER nightclub from March 1997 to 2000 hosted by the Sabretooth Clan. Here event was a center point of the history and foundations of the modern vampire subculture.

Mentor - On individual, usually an elder who actively takes on a student and teaches them the culture of the vampire world.

Meridians - Channels of energy through the subtle body akin to veins and arteries.

Mundane - The "normal" world which is not apart of and unfamiliar with vampire culture.

Need - The level of life-force energy needed to sate the "Thirst."

Nightside - The esoteric and spiritual side vampire world in contrast of the Dayside. This can also refer to "Vampire/Nightside" Family, lifestyle, magic, traditions and culture.

Otherkin - Commonly found around the vampire community are individuals who identify with another mythological archetype such as dragons, elves, faeries, etc. Some vampires consider themselves otherkin, while some do not.

Prana - Sandskrit for "Lifeforce energy" including prana, chi and ki.

Psychic Vampire - A vampire who feeds exclusively on lifeforce energy (chi, prane, ki) to fulfil their Need for a higher level of energy for the average human.

Real Vampire - An individual who identifies as a vampire usually sanguine vampire (blood) or psychic vampire (energy) or in some cases a lifestyle vampire. Also known as a Living Vampire.

Renfield's Syndrome - "Clinical vampirism" is a mental disorder where the individual has obsession with drinking blood.

Roleplayer - Someone who plays the roleplaying game Vampire the Masquerade, or pretends to be a Vampire..

Ronin - A highly solitary and or individualistic vampire who is not associated with any organization, clan, house or court.

Sacred Space - A place where the subtle reality and physical world interact. Usually created during rituals and ceremonies through magic and energy work.

Sabretooths - An individual who has had their fangs personally made by Father Sebastiaan and a member of the Sabretooth Clan.

Sabretooth Clan - The "Family" of individuals who are Sabretooths. The largest and one of the oldest clans in the vampire world. Founded in August 1995 as a "fangclub" for Father Sebastiaan's fang clients.

Sanguine - The Latin word for blood. In old terms this means "family" or "of the blood".

Sanguinarium - Was an international forum network of courts (local gatherings), households (covens), havens (sacred spaces) and businesses founded in 1995 by the Sabretooth Clan.

Sanguinarian - An individual who believes they need to drink physical human blood to sate their "Need."

Shielding - To block or prevent subtle energies, a protective technique learned by many vampires.

Strigoi Vii - "Living vampire witch" in Romanian a tradition of magick practiced by vampires inspired by tantra, chaos magic, Eastern religions and mentalism.

Sire - Coming from the game Vampire the Masquerade, this term means "maker", "parent" or "mentor" within the Vampire Community. Often looked down upon by serious vampires but is becoming more and more commonly used.

Scholars - Researchers who specialize in vampire myth and often the subculture. Examples include Dr. Gordon J Melton (The Vampire Book, Invisible Ink Press 2010), Katherine Ramsland (Piercing the Darkness, Harper Voyager 1988), Dax Stokes (The Vampire Historian) and Rosemary Ellen Guiley (Vampires Among Us, Pocket 1991).

Subtle Body - The Astral or "mirror" spiritual double of the physical body. This includes vital lifeforce (blood), chakras (organs), aura (skin) and meridians (veins and arteries), ba (personality) and ka (vital spark).

Subtle Reality - The spiritual world beyond the five senses including the astral and ethereal layers of reality.

Surface energy - The vital lifeforce energy radiated by the aura, usually just beyond the skin.

Surface feeding - To energetically feed upon the outer layers of the aura.

Sympathetic Vampirism - A temporary need for lifeforce of a non-vampire and psychic vampire condition created by being fed on too deeply over too long a period of time.

White Swan - A non-vampire who opposes Vampire Culture and lifestyle.

Vampire - Many definitions referring to individuals

Vampirism - Several definitions. 1. The act of feeding on lifeforce or blood from other individuals. 2. The philosophy of living as a vampire.

Vampire Culture (VC) - Is the world wide subculture of individuals who love or identify with the vampires archetype. It is also referred to as the Vampire Community.

Vampire World - 1. the entire vampire community and fandom. A documentary by Father Sebastiaan and Sean Fernald scheduled to be released in 2019.

Vampire the Masquerade - A roleplaying game which has highly influenced vampire culture. Published by White Wolf Entertainment in 1991.

Vampyre - The older Victorian spelling of vampire commonly used in the more old school vampire community. It was originally used to differentiate between lifestyle with a "Y" and fiction with an "I." However this spelling with a Y has become less and less common in the recent years.

#0167 - 310818 - C0 - 229/152/12 - PB - DID2291220